Baby's Best Chance

Parents' Handbook of Pregnancy and Baby Care

Fourth Edition

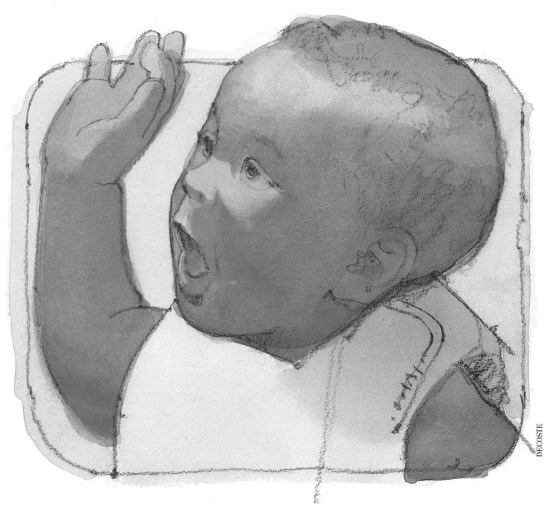

DECOSTE

Macmillan Canada

A Division of Canada Publishing Corporation
Toronto, Ontario, Canada

Canadian Cataloguing in Publication Data
Main entry under title:
Baby's best chance: parents' handbook of pregnancy and baby care

4th ed.
Includes index.
ISBN 0-7715-9060-1

1. Pregnancy. 2. Prenatal care. 3. Childbirth. 4. Infants — Care.

RG525.B33 1994   618.2'4   C93-095507-2

Macmillan Canada
A Division of Canada Publishing Corporation
29 Birch Avenue
Toronto, Ontario, Canada
M4V 1E2

Editorial co-ordinator: *Susan Girvan*
Production co-ordinator: *Lorraine Greey*

Cover photograph: *Hal Roth Photography*
Diapers courtesy of *Stork Diaper Service*

Printed in Canada
1 2 3 4 5 98 97 96 95 94

Table of Contents

Preface

This fourth edition of *Baby's Best Chance: Parents' Handbook of Pregnancy and Baby Care* follows three editions previously published by the British Columbia Ministry of Health. The first edition, published in early 1987, was a revised, enhanced version of the original (1979) *Baby's Best Chance* perinatal manual. In addition to a new magazine format, it offered a more comprehensive range of pregnancy and childbirth information, along with colour illustrations. New articles and further revision of the handbook resulted in the second edition in early 1989, and a third edition in 1991, which featured an expanded table of contents and an index. The fourth edition provides updated information building on the basis provided by earlier editions.

Many professionals within the British Columbia Ministry of Health were involved in selecting and reviewing information contained in this handbook. Thanks are extended to the contributors to all previous editions whose work has made this edition possible.

Thanks are also extended to the following individuals for their contribution to this edition:

Dr. Susan G. Albersheim, Clinical Assistant Professor, Department of Pediatrics, University of British Columbia, and British Columbia's Children's Hospital

Dr. Warren Bell, Family Physician, Salmon Arm, B.C.

Marianne Borup-Weston, Director of Publications, International Childbirth Education Association, Terrace, B.C.

Dr. Basil Boulton, Pediatrician, Victoria, B.C.

Marilyn Chung, Head Nurse, Special Care Nursery, Royal Columbian Hospital, New Westminster, B.C.

Freda Davis, La Leche League, Victoria, B.C.

Dr. Bill Ehman, Family Physician, Nanaimo, B.C.

Dr. Jan Friedman, Professor and Department Head of Medical Genetics, University of British Columbia

Debra Kent, British Columbia Drug and Poison Information Centre, Vancouver, B.C.

Dr. Ken Kolotyluk, President, Society of General Practitioners

Marty Layne, La Leche League, Victoria, B.C.

Marcina Levine, Education Director, Planned Parenthood Association of British Columbia

Dr. Verity Livingstone, Assistant Professor, Department of Family Practice, University of British Columbia

Suzanne McBride, Professional Liaison Representative, La Leche League, Powell River, B.C.

Lynn McLachlin, Prenatal Educator, Victoria, B.C.

Dr. Tom Martin, Obstetrician, Vancouver, B.C.

Dr. Margaret G. Norman, Director, C.G. Willis Screening Laboratory, Vancouver, B.C.

Bonnie Nilson, British Columbia Representative, International Childbirth Education Association, Castlegar, B.C.

Dr. Margaret Pendray, Neonatologist, Vancouver, B.C.

Dr. Sidney Segal, Pediatrician, Vancouver, B.C.

Barbara Selwood, Perinatal Co-ordinator, Vancouver Health Department, Vancouver, B.C.

Dr. Dorothy Shaw, President-Elect of the Society of Obstetricians and Gynecologists of Canada

Mr. and Mrs. Anthony Smith, President Couple, Serena, B.C.

Sharon Staseson, Program Director, British Columbia Reproductive Care Programme

Dr. Hugh Venables, Insurance Corporation of British Columbia

Sheila Welock, Product Safety Officer, Pacific Region, Consumer and Corporate Affairs, Canada

Practice Advisors and Special Interest Groups, Registered Nursing Association of British Columbia

Distributed in British Columbia through Pharmasave, Peoples Drug Mart, selected independent drug-stores, and selected health unit offices.

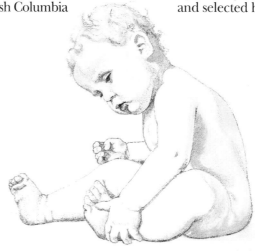

Introduction

Becoming a parent is an exciting life experience, especially if you are expecting your first child. Learning that you are soon to be a mother or father can produce many feelings — satisfaction, happiness, surprise, and anticipation, along with anxiety or concern about what lies in store. Such feelings are natural, for the pregnancy period and the first few months of caring for a new baby are often a time of great change.

Knowing what to expect can make the coming changes easier to handle and enjoy. That's where this handbook is designed to help. It contains more than 60 short, easy-to-read articles on a range of topics from the emotions you may be experiencing during the pregnancy to the way an infant develops physically and mentally in the first few months of life. You'll find clear, well-illustrated explanations of what happens to the mother during labour and childbirth, along with practical advice on how you can prepare. No matter what your personal, cultural, social, or religious background, you will find *Baby's Best Chance: Parents' Handbook of Pregnancy and Baby Care* a useful guide you can browse through or refer to as questions arise (a detailed table of contents and an index have been included to make information easier to find).

Important sources of information and support you can call on during this time are your friends and family members who may themselves be parents. Equally important are the qualified medical and helping professionals (ranging from community health and social workers to personal or spiritual counsellors) who possess the knowledge and experience needed to address your particular concerns. *Baby's Best Chance: Parents' Handbook of Pregnancy and Baby Care* provides suggestions on how to get the most from the professionals who are there to help. You will also find suggestions on where to obtain additional information or assistance.

Whether you are seeking information on what to expect during pregnancy or practical suggestions and support as you prepare for childbirth, you will find that one of the most valuable features of *Baby's Best Chance* is its up-to-date information. In each edition, articles and illustrations are updated to incorporate new information that is important to you.

Now That You're Pregnant... There Are Some Things You Should Know

So you're pregnant. What happens now? Just as no two people are exactly alike, so no two pregnancies are the same. But the things you do during your pregnancy definitely make a difference. By being aware of the physical and emotional changes occurring throughout your pregnancy and by taking advantage of pregnancy information and support, you can take care of your own future health and that of your baby.

To help you adjust to pregnancy and prepare for the birth of your child, many communities offer prenatal classes. Pregnancy and birth information is also available at libraries, which carry books and magazines on the subject.

If you can, you should take advantage of whatever help and support is available. But maybe you live in an isolated community or you have a demanding job or a large family to look after. Maybe you don't have time to read a lot and you dislike classes of any kind. Whatever your situation, the following list is worth considering. It offers some basic tips on things to do and things to avoid while pregnant. It also provides some highlights of this handbook and tells you

CHAPMAN

6

where you can look to find out more about many of these subjects.

- Seeing a doctor for early prenatal care is essential.
- Be sure to tell the health care practitioners you visit, including your dentist, that you are pregnant. If anyone wishes to prescribe a medication or carry out a procedure, ask what effect this may have on you or your baby.
- Drugs or medications of any kind during pregnancy should be taken only with your doctor's knowledge and advice (see the article "Alcohol and Other Drugs" on p. 24).
- X-rays should be avoided, including dental X-rays, unless they are critical to treatment. Talk to your doctor before undergoing any X-rays.
- Eat a well-balanced diet every day. It should include a variety of nutritious foods, as listed in the "Food Guide for Pregnancy and Breastfeeding" (see p. 16).
- Swimming and walking are excellent forms of exercise for a healthy pregnant woman (see the article "Physical Activity throughout Pregnancy" on p. 21).
- If you smoke, now is the time to quit. Every time you smoke tobacco, the unborn baby's heart rate increases, and the supply of oxygen, which the baby needs in order to develop, decreases (see "Alcohol and Other Drugs" on p. 24).
- Any alcohol you consume reaches the baby. The safe level of intake is not known, so it is best not to consume any alcohol while pregnant (see p. 24 for more information).
- If you are a heavy coffee drinker, you should cut down to four or fewer cups a day. Evidence shows that caffeine crosses the placenta into the baby's circulation and that the baby's system is unable to process it (see p. 26 for more information).
- Irritability and mood changes are common during pregnancy. Be sure to schedule activities that you find relaxing and enjoyable.
- If you suffer from nausea and/or vomiting, try eating small amounts of food every one to two hours, rather than larger meals three times a day (see the article "Staying Comfortable during Pregnancy" on p. 35).
- To help lessen the chance of leg cramps and prevent varicose veins, sit with your feet raised as often as possible (see p. 37 for more information).
- Be sure to maintain good posture at all times and avoid wearing high-heeled shoes. This will help prevent backache (see p. 37 for more information). Also, lie down and stand up carefully and avoid sudden changes in position (i.e., from lying to standing). This will prevent lowered blood pressure (called postural hypotension), which may cause dizziness or fainting.
- Good dental care (proper daily flossing and brushing) is important during pregnancy. Hormonal changes can lead to red, infected gums (pregnancy gingivitis) if plaque is left on your teeth.

- If you have had contact with anyone who has rubella (German measles), notify your doctor. If you contract this disease, especially in the first six weeks of pregnancy, there is a risk that your baby could develop congenital heart disease, blindness, deafness, and/or mental retardation.
- If you are sleepy, give in to the urge to nap and be sure to get plenty of rest.
- Unless your doctor advises against it, there is no reason why you can't make love during pregnancy (see the article "And What about Sex?" on p. 29).
- Nothing definite is known about the effects on mother and baby of substances such as paints, varnishes, paint removers, pesticides, or many cleansers but there is suggestive evidence of possible harm. Since ingesting or inhaling large amounts of these substances may be harmful, it is a good idea to limit your contact with them.
- Since cats may carry toxoplasmosis, a parasite that could harm your unborn child if you become infected while you are pregnant, wear rubber gloves to change the cat's litter. Wash your hands when you are done. Better yet, have someone else take care of the litter box during your pregnancy.
- Limit any time you spend in a sauna, hot tub, or hot bath to ten minutes (less if you are feeling uncomfortable). It is also a good idea to reduce the temperature to below 38.9°C (102°F). There should be a second adult present in case you feel faint or dizzy (see the article "Saunas/Hot Tubs/Hot Baths: Approach with Caution" on p. 26).

Whatever your situation, health care professionals have the ability and equipment available to provide excellent care. They are trained to deal with difficulties that you may encounter during pregnancy, labour, and delivery. Like most women, you want to have the healthiest possible pregnancy and the healthiest possible baby. So in_____ n to taking care of yourself, you should seek extra atte_____ om your doctor or referral to another health care pro____ ı-al, if you:

- are underweight or overweight,
- have had problems with a previous pregnancy (e.g., your baby was premature or weighed less than 2500 g [5 lb. 8 oz.]),
- have diabetes, high blood pressure, heart disease, kidney disease, or anemia,
- are over 35 or under 16 years of age,
- have become pregnant within one year of your last pregnancy,
- are carrying more than one baby,
- have had a Caesarean birth or uterine surgery,
- have an alcohol, smoking, or drug habit,
- are under severe emotional stress, or
- are very physically active at work, at home, or in your leisure activities.

Support: A Few Thoughts

Pregnancy is a time of emotional and physical change, so it's natural to need extra support — both practical and emotional — from one's partner or a close friend. Attending prenatal classes, assisting during labour, or simply listening to each other and talking about the changes that are occurring can be a source of great comfort and can help make the pregnancy a more worry-free time. It's also the reason why nowadays the role of the "support person" is understood and valued more than ever by pregnant women, prenatal experts, and medical professionals alike.

Maybe you've thought about offering your support but are hesitant because you're unsure of how to help. In fact, there are several important and rewarding ways that you can get involved.

• Share a healthy lifestyle by establishing a comfortable routine and finding activities and social situations that support a healthy pregnancy.

• Participate in those physical exercises that require a partner.

• Practise massage and relaxation techniques that will help the mother-to-be stay comfortable throughout pregnancy.

• Offer emotional support by listening and being there during those times when you are feeling unsure of your new role.

• Accompany the mother-to-be to appointments (this is especially important if you are planning to be present during labour).

• Help rehearse for labour by practising breathing and relaxation techniques as well as comfort positions.

• As labour draws near, help get ready for the hospital and prepare for the mother-to-be's absence at home and/or at work.

• Be a birth companion by sharing the labour, helping practise relaxation techniques, and giving support and encouragement.

Once you've made the decision to be a support person, how can you prepare yourself? A good way to start is by reading some of the relevant articles right here in *Baby's Best Chance*! "Experiencing Fatherhood" (p. 10), "Getting It Together to Be a Father" (p. 12), "Staying Comfortable during Pregnancy" (p. 35), "Rehearsing for Labour" (p. 51), "What to Take to the Hospital" (p. 55), and "When the Time Comes: Comfort Positions during Labour" (p. 58) all contain useful information for support persons. As well, if you would like to learn more about how a baby develops and what happens during childbirth, the articles "Baby in Progress" (p. 31) and "Giving Birth" (p. 60) will tell you what you need to know.

Beyond reading, you can prepare by simply spending time together. Getting involved in the pregnancy will help you find out what kind of care is needed. Above all, remember it is understanding, support, and companionship that will make the difference.

However you become involved, you can be sure that you have the support of the various health care professionals who are there to help. By working in partnership with these professionals, you will go a long way towards providing the best possible care and support. And you will be rewarded by sharing in a joyous and fulfilling life experience.

Choosing a Health Care Provider

It is important to contact a doctor as soon as you think you are pregnant. If you don't have a doctor, here are some suggestions on how to find one.

• Ask friends for recommendations.

• Call the College of Physicians and Surgeons or the College of Family Physicians for names of doctors who are taking new patients in your neighbourhood. If you live in a fairly large community, you can also consult the local medical society.

• Call doctors' offices and ask the questions that are important to you (e.g., Is the doctor interested in working with couples who are pregnant? Does the doctor have experience working with single mothers? What is the doctor's policy regarding phone calls, home visits, and frequency and length of office visits? What is the on-call coverage, especially at the time of birth?). Remember to ask about birth options, hospital facilities, and any other concerns that you have.

• Ask another health care professional (e.g., a nurse or childbirth educator) for recommendations.

It is important to have a doctor with whom you can communicate and feel comfortable.

What to Expect at Prenatal Visits

Throughout most of the pregnancy, you will be seeing your doctor approximately once a month. These visits will increase to once every one to two weeks from 36 weeks on as you move closer to delivery. Your doctor may ask you to come in for extra visits if your condition warrants extra care. If you have special concerns, you may wish to make more frequent visits as well.

You should have enough time with your doctor to have all your questions answered and concerns dealt with. Be prepared, even if you have to write your questions down. If you are visiting the doctor for the first time, be ready to provide your health history. It is especially important for a partner or support person to be involved in the early visits since both of you will be working in partnership with your doctor.

At your initial visit, or soon after, your doctor may want to do a pap smear. Blood tests may also be done initially, especially with a first pregnancy. They may be done once or twice more at later stages in the pregnancy.

At each visit, you will be asked to give a urine sample, and you will be weighed. Your doctor will also take your blood pressure and examine and measure your abdomen. The doctor will be able to hear the baby's heartbeat at about the eighteenth to twentieth week. In many cases, the heartbeat can be heard much earlier if an electronic listening device is used. Ask if you can listen, too.

In addition to checking your physical health and the health of your baby, the doctor may wish to discuss the following topics:
- any physical concerns and any problems you may be having,
- your eating and exercise habits,
- stresses in your life,
- use of drugs during pregnancy (including over-the-counter drugs, cigarettes, alcohol, etc.),
- prenatal information: It is important to sign up for prenatal classes as early as possible in your pregnancy and/or to check out other resources in your community that you feel comfortable with (e.g., singles' programs).
- ultrasound: Ultrasound is a scan that uses sound waves to show the development of the baby in the uterus. Ultrasound is not a routine procedure. Its most common uses in pregnancy are to confirm pregnancy, to establish the estimated date of delivery, to detect certain developmental problems in the baby, to assess the maturity of the fetus, to detect the baby's position, and to assess the condition and position of the placenta.
- genetic counselling: If you have a family history of babies with congenital abnormalities, or if you are 35 years old or older, this is an important topic to talk about with your doctor.
- RhoGAM: This is an injection usually given to women who have Rh (rhesus) negative blood. It is given around the twenty-eighth week of pregnancy and after delivery. (You will find out if you are Rh negative from the initial blood tests you have done. Your doctor will discuss your specific factors with you.)
- glucose screen: This blood test may be done between the twenty-fourth and twenty-eighth weeks of pregnancy to detect a form of diabetes (glucose intolerance) that may develop during pregnancy.
- non-stress test: The doctor will evaluate the baby's heart-rate pattern by using an electronic monitor. This test is done near the time of delivery, especially if the baby is overdue.
- fetal movement counting: This is done to check your baby's health or if you notice a decrease in the baby's movements.

While the knowledge and expertise of your doctor and other health care professionals is important, you and your partner or support person contribute by maintaining a healthy lifestyle and becoming better informed about pregnancy and childbirth.

Experiencing Fatherhood

Fatherhood and the role of the male have undergone some significant changes over the past decade. Today's father is more likely to be actively participating in the delivery room as opposed to pacing the floor in a waiting area. And when mother and baby are home, he is likely to be changing diapers and making dinner — pitching in to care for the new family member.

It's a new experience for both mother and father. But for many men, just holding a baby in their arms is traumatic, never mind changing a diaper or burping a baby. At least, that was the experience of the new father who tells his story here. In some ways his story is unique, but in many other ways his experiences and feelings will ring true in the hearts and minds of so many first-time fathers:

My ride on the emotional roller-coaster known as fatherhood began with a phone call from my wife. I was living during the week at an apartment in the city where I worked and commuted home on weekends. The phone call was just one in an evening ritual of calls that made the weekly separation bearable for my wife and me — and extremely profitable for the telephone company.

Part way through our conversation, Maureen mentioned that she was "late." I asked her where she was going. "No, I mean late this month," she elaborated. "So I've made a doctor's appointment." There was some silence, probably about a dollar's worth or so before I weakly sought further clarification and confirmation of the situation. "We *are* talking about what I think we are, right?" I ventured. I heard a small sigh of exasperation: "Bruce, you might as well face it. I'm pregnant!"

The doctor's appointment confirmed what we already knew, and an ultrasound a couple of weeks later informed us that we were about six weeks pregnant. I asked Maureen how big the baby would be at this stage. Probably not a good thing for me to know because I couldn't look at grapes or peanuts for weeks after hearing her answer. I became obsessed with babies and everything to do with them. As fate would have it, *Life* magazine printed a cover article that month on the growth and development of the human baby. The photo-essay was so incredibly fascinating, I picked up several copies of the magazine and considered it a potential collector's item.

For the next while, weekends were spent checking out garage and yard sales that promised lots of baby clothes and toys. We went mostly to price things because we were just at the outset of our pregnancy and didn't want to jump the gun. However, a deal is a deal, and we ended up buying many so-called basic baby items that we just couldn't pass up. At most of these sales, there were children — infants and toddlers — of all ages and sizes. I would ask the parents how old the kids were and what they could do at that age. The answers gave me an idea of what we would be getting and when. The proud, doting parents took the opportunity to gush about their precious offspring to a perfect stranger, who was willing to pay ten bucks for a nursery mobile that they no longer needed.

I waited several months before telling anyone at work that we were pregnant, probably because I was still somewhat in shock. Also, I figured that if there were any type of problem there was no sense dragging everyone else into it. I was still having a tough time coming to terms with a development that was going to have such a major impact on our lives. Millions of ideas and concerns would race through my mind whenever I was alone with my thoughts. Life insurance, job security, birth defects, new car, new house, cloth versus disposable diapers — these were just a few of the things I pondered over the next several months.

After a while, Maureen began to actually look pregnant. Her appearance began to bother her when she was unable to fit into some of her clothes. I told her that one of the unavoidable consequences of getting pregnant was getting a bit of a belly. She sarcastically thanked me for my concern and understanding and ran into the bedroom crying. I learned then that another unavoidable consequence of pregnancy is rapid and radical mood swings. I realized that I would have to tread softly around the home front in order to avoid touching off an outburst.

As summer and our pregnancy marched on, we took a trip to California. While playing at being tourists, we visited several up-scale baby shops to *look* at $1200 baby quilts, $200 outfits, and $25 rattles among other decadent items. Upon learning of our baby-to-be, one store clerk asked what we were having — a boy or a girl. When I said we didn't know yet, she looked at me as if I didn't know what planet I was on. Later, we sat on a park bench and watched all of the so-called family units walk by with little ones in tow and wondered what our family would look like on our next trip.

It was some time later that Maureen began to tell me she could feel the baby move. In fact, she could feel the baby move a lot. All hours of the day and night, the baby would be doing the fetal lambada. Every time I would race over to feel the baby, he would stop and probably hide over at the other side of the womb. However, by all accounts, a baby that moved a lot was a healthy baby.

But as pregnant mothers are wont to do, Maureen began to worry. "What if the baby can't stop moving — you know, what if there's some type of problem?" she asked. "Don't be ridiculous," I would reply. "You're just being paranoid. Go to sleep." Maureen would settle down and fall asleep, and for the rest of the night, or for at least a few hours, I would lie in bed and think, "What if he can't stop moving?" I realized then that one of the most important roles for the father is to harbour the worries and fears in order to keep the mother as stress-free as possible.

Some weeks later, while we were nestled in bed with Maureen's belly pushed up against the small of my back, I felt some tiny little movements. I realized that for the very first time I was feeling the baby. If he was anything like his daddy, our baby was probably looking around for a little late-night snack.

The rest of the pregnancy moved along quite rapidly, for me anyway. Maureen slowly changed shape; she continued to exercise and plan her food choices. As we got closer to our due date, we gathered more baby furniture, equipment, and other paraphernalia. We accumulated enough clothes to dress several babies of all shapes and sizes. I was able to spend lots of time in toy stores and didn't have to worry about someone from work seeing me checking out the train sets.

Our due date came and went, and we began to become more anxious. When was this baby going to be born? I wanted to put a face to my image of our little baby. By two weeks after the due date, I began thinking we were going to have to register the child for kindergarten by proxy. False labour pains no longer caused me to run for the suitcase and the car keys.

It was late one night (of course) that Maureen woke me up and told me she thought we would be going soon. She had experienced steady pains for a few hours and the interval was becoming much shorter. I had done a lot of reading up on labour and how to be a good birthing partner, and a few weeks before we had toured the hospital. I felt alert, prepared, anxious, and, of course, terrified. We notified the hospital that we were on our way, and within a few minutes we had pulled up in front of the hospital entrance. We were soon checked in, and the most emotionally draining day of our lives was about to begin.

The labour went on for several hours, with all of the different stages seeming to blend into one long, difficult process. That night, after 27 hours of steady labour and about 52 hours of off-and-on pains, we gave birth to a nine-pound, one-ounce boy. The first act of our newborn son was to pee in the face of the doctor who had handled the forceps. Rather than viewing the act as his own personal comment on the experience of being forced into this new, strange world, we were pleased to see this as proof positive that his plumbing was performing properly.

As a new father, I found it difficult not to count toes and fingers and to make sure everything else that was sup-

posed to be there was there — and was present in the appropriate quantity. I carried him out to see his grandparents as if he were a fragile treasure. My back ached as a result of the physical tension of the delivery and the stress of carrying a baby for the first time. The drive home was not particularly memorable. I was busy thinking of how Maureen was doing after a tough delivery and how the baby looked the first time I saw him. When I was finally able to crawl into bed, I was still so pumped up it took hours to fall asleep.

The fourth trimester, as it is called, has probably been the toughest of all — for all three of us. Greggory is the king of the castle and he knew it right from the first few days. Our house has been completely taken over with his stuff — strollers (we had to get a bigger one because he had grown out of the first one by the second month), crib, super swing (no home should be without one), toys, change table (although every bit of loose change goes towards more baby paraphernalia), bassinet, and playpen.

Maureen is on maternity leave, and every day is absolutely full with feedings, baths, naps, and the daily laundry. Evenings are spent keeping the baby occupied — rumours of babies sleeping a lot have proven to be extremely exaggerated. Maureen is breastfeeding, so each time Greggory looks at her it's with a great big smile — she is his own private dairy. I earn my place by holding him and carrying him around and patting his back to get the burps up. Sometimes I bounce him on my knee as his own personal carnival ride. The time to fret and worry about getting ready for fatherhood is over. It's here. Now the time has come to worry and wonder why this baby never sleeps.

Colic is a misleading word. It really should be a four-letter word. Whenever anyone hears that you have a colicky baby, they usually cancel any plans for a visit and run the other way. Not that I blame them. I used to be the type that would become nauseated at the sound of a crying infant, even if it was in a large grocery or department store. Now, as a father, when our precious jewel is screaming his lungs out because of that terrible five-letter word, I cradle him on my shoulder or across my lap to try to calm his pains and his crying. Our baby's cries do not cause me severe mind trauma as the cries of other infants did. As a father, you quickly develop an immunity to the sounds of screams. Concerns for the cause and efforts to relieve the offending pains take over.

Greggory has become such a special part of our lives that it is now hard to imagine life without him. We have developed special little nicknames for him, depending on what he has been up to. Often, he is Winnie-the-Pooh, usually in the morning and occasionally in the evening. Sometimes I call him Li'l Grabber or Mr. Smiley. He shows us something new every day and challenges me as a father to meet his new demands and needs. Before he came along, I had only a nodding interest in issues such as child care and the school system and would listen politely — stifling a few yawns — while listening to other people prattle on about the topics. Now I read and seek out every bit of information on both issues and have formed strong opinions on what I want for our child.

A baby will do a lot of things to you, and on you. I have been peed on several times, spit up on, and worse. There is nothing in the world to match the three a.m. feeling of a baby's overflow of warm milk running down your back after a too successful attempt at burping, then not being able to properly wash off because the sink is full of dirty diapers. Yes, a baby will do a lot of things to you. But most of all, a baby will grow on you, and fatherhood will grow on you. I suppose it's not for everyone, but for me, now that I am well into my life as a father, I wouldn't want it any other way.

Getting It Together to Be a Father

If you're like many first-time fathers nowadays, you probably expect to be in attendance for the birth of your child. You probably also expect to play a significant role in child care after the baby is born. But maybe you're asking yourself, "Just what am I letting myself in for with these expectations?" or maybe you have some unspoken concerns about your role in this whole business of becoming a father. If so, you're still like many first-time fathers, believe it or not.

Recently, an American psychologist interviewed more than 200 expectant and new fathers of various ages, from all walks of life. To his surprise, he found that many of them shared similar fears and concerns — things they hadn't spoken about with anyone else. Here are the seven main concerns the psychologist identified.

Queasiness: The most universal concern was the fear of not being able to handle the sight of blood and of not being able to be present for the childbirth without fainting or becoming nauseous.

Increased responsibility: More than 80 per cent of the fathers who were interviewed agreed that a big concern was having to support a dependent child and, in some cases, losing all or part of a second income if the mother had been working previously and planned not to return to work immediately. Being the *sole* breadwinner for a family has never been easy, and nowadays it is harder than ever.

Dealing with medical professionals: The sheer quantity of medical know-how that a doctor brings to the delivery room was intimidating to some fathers. Men who were uncomfortable dealing with a subject about which they were

somewhat ignorant to begin with were put off even more by the clinical manner of busy professionals who wanted to concentrate on their main job: getting the baby delivered safely and keeping the mother healthy, too.

Uncertain paternity: Many men admitted to having nagging doubts about not being the actual father of their child. Others expressed concern about the hospital mixing up their baby with someone else's. In most cases, these doubts were based less on any real concern that the wife or partner had been unfaithful than on a general insecurity brought on by being part of something as monumental as the creation of life.

Losing partner and/or child: The thought of a disaster in childbirth that could result in the death of the mother or infant or in a handicap (e.g., brain damage) to the infant was a widespread and quite understandable fear. The fact that death in childbirth was for centuries a frequent and tragic occurrence may help to explain why so many men experience this fear.

Being replaced: As a pregnant woman turns inward, thinking more about the new life inside her, it is natural for the father to feel left out. Some men even admitted to feeling jealous at the shift in the mother's attention away from themselves and towards the growing baby. With all the stresses that life today imposes on a relationship, and with what

CHAPMAN

we know about divorce rates and marriage breakdowns, the concern about losing the relationship is a natural and understandable one.

Personal mortality: Several men, especially those who had already attended the childbirth, said they felt closer to their own deaths as a result of having been so closely involved with the beginnings of life. These feelings about human fragility and their own deaths often hit first-time fathers especially hard. Until they had had a child, first-time fathers could more easily think of themselves as the young generation of their family, with time to spare and likely to outlive older family members.[1]

So, supposing you share some of these concerns, the question is, "What do you do about them?" Perhaps it will help to realize that, in the case of some worries, the statistics are all on your side. For instance, an extremely small percentage of men actually do suffer from queasiness during childbirth. And although people sometimes focus on all the possible medical problems that could occur during childbirth, the fact is that modern medicine has brought the rates of death and injury among women in childbirth and their babies to almost zero. This is particularly true for the mother who has had a healthy pregnancy involving a good diet, lots of rest, and plenty of the right kind of exercise.

The most important thing you can do for yourself, however, is to talk about your feelings to your wife or partner. Far from making the pregnancy more burdensome for her, knowing what's going on in your mind will probably make her feel closer to you. Talk to your partner if you:
- find visits to the doctor difficult,
- worry about being replaced in her affections,
- fear losing her or the baby in childbirth, or
- feel left out of this major event that's happening in your lives and uncertain about your role as the father.

By talking about these feelings, you will reassure her of your love and your desire to be involved at a time when she needs all of your support (whether she realizes it or not). You may find that by talking it over the things you thought

were bothering you were simply covering up other unidentified worries. If this is the case, getting a handle on the real causes of concern will be the first step in dealing with them. Telling yourself you should be strong enough to handle your fears and concerns on your own can just end up making life more difficult for you. It can also make it harder to establish the close emotional connections you and your partner both need at this time.

At the same time, don't be too proud to accept help from other people. Maybe her parents or yours are looking for some way to help out — perhaps financially. Maybe you have friends who'll put a little time into helping you get a room ready for the baby or tune up your car and adjust the brakes so you'll be prepared for that drive to the hospital when the time comes.

There are, as well, dozens of practical things you can do to attack some of your worries head on. If money is a concern, sit down and take a look at your finances. Then draw up a budget and make some tough decisions. Maybe you should even think about insurance or about drawing up a will. If you feel awkward and left out of the whole pregnancy experience, take a look at ways to get involved. Many of the articles in this book were written with the pregnant woman in mind, but there are some that present things for you to think about, too. Check out the articles "What Kind of Parent Will I Make?," "A Guide for Birth Companions," "Protecting Your Baby from Harm," "Baby on Board: Car Seat Safety," and "Getting Baby Equipment." If you want to know all about the ins and outs of feeding a baby or how the baby develops, take a look at the articles on those subjects, too. It may help you feel more prepared when you deal with the doctors and other health care professionals.

Finally, take a moment to consider that, despite any appearance to the contrary, the role of father is still one of the most respected and valued in our society. Sure, that role is changing, and you will be called on to involve yourself in child rearing in ways your grandfather probably could never have imagined — changing diapers, fetching the groceries, making the meals, or doing the laundry. However, the basic respect and authority that fathers have always enjoyed are still present. You'll discover it in the way your family, your friends, and even the people you work with treat you. They will expect more of you, trusting more in your maturity, your sense of responsibility, and your capacity to make level-headed decisions. You'll feel it in the appreciation your wife or partner has for the way you pick up the slack when her energy is low. And you'll feel it perhaps most of all when your yet-unborn baby becomes a toddler, rushing to greet you at the end of a long day with a welcome that leaves you in no doubt you're the number one guy!

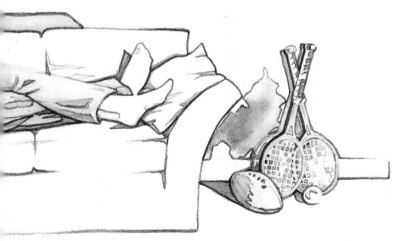

[1] **Jerrold Lee Shapiro, "The Expectant Father,"** *Psychology Today*, **January, 1987: 36.**

Over 35 and Expecting

CHAPMAN

A growing number of couples have chosen to postpone having a family until they feel they are financially and emotionally ready. These couples find that delaying childbirth has many advantages. Greater maturity often means:
• greater financial stability,
• a more stable relationship with one another,
• stronger friendships, and
• more experience in coping with stress and change.

Also, older mothers tend to have a broader perspective on pregnancy and parenting. Some of them have pursued careers and may be less concerned about "what might have been." They may also be more inclined to learn about nutritional needs, to get the rest they need, and to look for information on parenting and discipline rather than simply reacting to their child's behaviour.

Despite these advantages, beginning parenting later in life presents challenges. A major adjustment in lifestyle may be required, such as living on one income instead of two. The mother who has pursued a career and decides to remain at home after the baby is born may have to deal with feelings of resentment or jealousy if her partner continues to advance in his career while she devotes her time to looking after the baby. Her partner, on the other hand, may worry about losing his relationship with her after years of being just the two of them.

The most frequent concern of older expectant parents is the idea that women over 35 are too old and that pregnancy, labour, and delivery will be much harder for them than for younger women. Many doctors are now saying that age is less important than a woman's health, nutrition, medical history, and the quality of medical care she receives.

There are, however, some medical risks that women over 35 should be aware of. Older women are at more risk of having a baby with Down syndrome or other chromosomal problems. There are currently two tests that can be performed to detect such abnormalities. Amniocentesis is usually performed at 14 to 17 weeks. It involves the removal of a small amount of fluid from the mother's abdomen under ultrasound guidance. Results take about three and a half weeks. The major risk with amniocentesis is to increase the chance of miscarriage by about one in 200. Chorionic villus sampling (CVS) is usually performed between 10 and 12 weeks of pregnancy. It involves the removal of a small amount of placental tissue. This is done either vaginally or through the abdomen, again under ultrasound guidance. Results take about two and a half weeks. The major risk of CVS is to increase the chance of miscarriage by about one in 100. It also appears to be associated with about a one in 1000 risk of a limb defect.

The vast majority of couples will be reassured by the results of these tests. When abnormalities are found, further counselling is provided to give information on all aspects of the options available to them. The couple can then decide whether to continue the pregnancy.

A higher incidence of miscarriage is a further risk for older mothers. This is partly because older mothers are more likely to carry defective embryos. However, it is the health of the woman's reproductive system, not her age, that determines whether her pregnancy will continue to term. In fact, important as it is for couples to be aware of the risks of beginning parenting later in life, it is equally important to remember that problem pregnancies are the exception, not the rule. With good health, a positive attitude, and thorough prenatal care, the odds are overwhelmingly in favour of giving birth to a healthy baby.

Rating Your Prenatal Lifestyle

Read the following statements to identify aspects of your lifestyle that you could alter or change to benefit yourself and your baby.

Could I Improve?

I am a nonsmoker
(of cigarettes or marijuana).
yes ❑   no ❑

I take no drugs,
except those that are
recommended by my doctor.
yes ❑   no ❑

I eat regularly throughout
the day.
yes ❑   no ❑

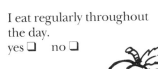

I don't drink alcoholic beverages.
yes ❑   no ❑

I take time
to relax
each day.
yes ❑   no ❑

I am making myself more
informed about pregnancy,
birth, and parenting.
yes ❑   no ❑

I get enough sleep.
yes ❑   no ❑

I exercise regularly.
yes ❑   no ❑

I am receiving regular prenatal care
from a doctor.
yes ❑   no ❑

I limit my coffee
intake to no more
than four cups a day.
yes ❑   no ❑

I have friends and family to help me out.
yes ❑   no ❑

I have seen my dentist since getting
pregnant.
yes ❑   no ❑

ORESNIK

Food Guide for Pregnancy and Breastfeeding

The amount of food you need every day depends on your age, body size, and activities. That's why there is a range of servings for each food group.
- Enjoy a variety of foods from the four food groups every day.
- Eat regularly (three meals and three snacks) every day.

Enjoy eating well, being active, and feeling good about yourself!

Grain Products (8 to 10 servings per day)

Choose whole-grain and enriched products more often.

One serving:
1 slice bread
175 mL cooked cereal (3/4 cup)
30 g ready-to-eat cereal (1.25 oz.)
50 g pancake or waffle batter (1/4 cup)
1 tortilla or roti (15 cm / 6")
small bannock or scone
4 graham wafers
6 soda crackers

Two servings:
1 hamburger or hot dog bun
1 roll or muffin
1 bagel, pita or English muffin
250 mL pasta or rice (1 cup)

Vegetables and Fruit (6 to 10 servings per day)

Choose dark green and orange vegetables and fruit more often.

One serving:
1 medium-size vegetable or fruit
  (potato, carrot, tomato, peach, apple, orange, or banana)
125 mL vegetables or fruit (fresh, frozen, or canned) (1/2 cup)
250 mL salad (1 cup)
125 mL juice (1/2 cup)
60 mL dried apricots, prunes, or raisins (1/4 cup)

Milk Products (3 to 4 servings per day)

Choose lower fat milk products (skim, 1%, or 2%) more often.

One serving:
250 mL milk or buttermilk (1 cup)
50 g cheese (3"x1"x1")
2 slices processed cheese
175 mL yogurt (3/4 cup)
125 mL evaporated milk (1/2 cup)
75 mL instant skim milk powder (1/3 cup)
60 mL Parmesan cheese (1/4 cup)

Meat and Alternatives (2 to 3 servings per day)

Choose leaner meats, poultry, and fish as well as dried peas, beans, and lentils more often.

One serving:
50-100 g cooked meat, poultry or fish (2-4 oz.)
50-100 g canned fish (2-4 oz.)
1-2 eggs
125-250 mL cooked dried beans, peas, or lentils
  (1/2-1 cup)
100 g tofu (1/3 cup)
30 mL peanut butter or tahini (2 tbsp)
60 mL nuts or seeds (1/4 cup)

Other Foods

Taste and enjoyment can also come from other foods and beverages that are not part of the four food groups. Some of these foods are higher in fat or calories, so use these in moderation. Other foods include butter, cream, mayonnaise, sweets, cake, cookies, pastry, and potato chips.

*Adapted from Canada's Guide to Healthy Eating

The Six Steps to Healthy Eating For Pregnancy

When you are pregnant, your nutritional needs are very important. Healthy eating helps you look and feel better and have more energy, and increases your chances of having a healthy baby.

How do your eating habits measure up?

Follow these steps to find out:

Step 1: **Write down** everything you ate and drank yesterday. Include all meals, drinks, and snacks.

Morning:	Mid-morning:
Noon:	Mid-afternoon:
Supper:	Evening:

Step 2: **Find** the foods you ate yesterday in the food groups in the "Food Guide for Pregnancy and Breastfeeding" on the opposite page.

Step 3: **Estimate** the number of servings you ate of each food, and record below:

Grain Products: _____

Milk and Milk Products: _____

Vegetables and Fruit: _____

Meat and Alternatives: _____

Step 4: **Compare** your totals to the "Food Guide for Pregnancy and Breastfeeding."

Check the boxes below that apply to you:

❑ I ate the recommended number of servings in all four food groups.

❑ I ate less than the recommended number of servings in the four food groups. I need to eat more:

      ❑ Grain Products

      ❑ Vegetables and Fruit

      ❑ Milk Products

      ❑ Meat and Alternatives

Step 5: **Plan** how you will eat more of the foods you need.

Example: I need to eat more vegetables and fruit ... I will pack some raw vegetables in my lunch and have a large glass of juice at breakfast.

Your Plan: _____

_____

_____

Step 6: **Look at** the boxes below listing foods that are good sources of iron, folacin, calcium, and fibre — all needed in generous amounts during pregnancy.

Go back to your own food list and circle any of these foods that you ate yesterday.

Sources of Important Nutrients During Pregnancy

	Iron-rich Foods	*Folacin-rich Foods*	*Calcium-rich Foods*	*Fibre-rich Foods*
Grain Products	whole-grain cereals enriched cereals			bran cereal bran muffin oatmeal whole-wheat bread
Vegetables and Fruit	broccoli prune juice dried fruit raisins	broccoli cauliflower corn Romaine lettuce peas cabbage bananas orange juice	broccoli	broccoli corn peas spinach potatoes prunes apples
Milk Products			milk buttermilk cheese yogurt skim milk powder	
Meat and Alternatives	red meat liverwurst eggs (yolks) dried beans dried peas lentils pumpkin seeds sunflower seeds	kidney beans baked beans lentils peanuts sunflower seeds peanut butter	sardines salmon with bones tofu made with calcium	dried beans lentils peanuts

This chart is a reminder to choose these foods daily.

Now, in six steps you have compared your own eating to the "Food Guide for Pregnancy and Breastfeeding," planned any changes needed, and checked good food sources of iron, folacin, calcium, and fibre. You've done the "ground work" for healthy eating during pregnancy! For more details and answers to some common food-related questions, read on to pages 19 and 20.

What Should I Eat When I'm Pregnant?

Like most pregnant women, you need more food energy, more nutrients, and plenty of fluids. Your energy needs can by met by increasing the number of servings from each food group. Your special nutritional challenge is to get enough calcium, iron, and folacin. See the chart on p. 18 for good sources of these nutrients and fiber. Women who are planning a pregnancy or are in the first three months of pregnancy, should discuss folacin supplements with their doctor. The Society of Obstetricians and Gynecologists of Canada and the Canadian College of Medical Geneticists recommend taking a .4 mg folacin supplement daily.

Here, a registered dietitian-nutritionist answers some common food-related questions:

Why is it important to eat well during pregnancy?

Nutritionist: Your baby is built from the nutrients in the foods you eat. From conception on, your baby depends on you to provide a daily supply of healthy foods. By 12 weeks (the end of the first trimester), your baby will have all the systems and organs that a full-term baby would have. During the second trimester, your appetite usually increases, and the amount of food that you and your baby need increases. By the third trimester, most babies will weigh between 1 and 1.5 kg (2 and 3 lb.) and will gain about 30 g (1 oz.) per day for the remaining three months. It's important that you eat well and gain enough weight during pregnancy for your baby to develop and reach a healthy birth weight.

How is a woman supposed to eat all the food recommended in the "Food Guide for Pregnancy and Breastfeeding?"

Nutritionist: A good look at the serving sizes listed in the food guide can be reassuring. For example, a muffin and a hamburger bun are each equal to two servings of grain products. A typical serving of pasta (375 mL / 1 1/2 cups) equals three servings. A cup of juice (250 mL) equals two servings of vegetables and fruit.
- Women with small appetites should aim for the lower end of the range of number of servings.
- Very physically active women should aim for the upper end of the range.

- During the second and third trimesters, many women find they are more comfortable eating small amounts of food throughout the day rather than three large meals.
- Try not to skip a meal, particularly breakfast. Even a glass of milk and some crackers will get you started for the day.

How much weight should I gain during my pregnancy?

Nutritionist: Weight gain should be gradual. You may wish to discuss this with your doctor. If your pre-pregnancy weight is within a healthy range, the appropriate weight gain is 11 to 16 kg (25 to 35 lb.). If you are underweight before pregnancy, or if you are a teenager, a healthy weight gain is 13 to 18 kg (28 to 40 lb.). For women who are overweight before pregnancy, a 7 to 11.5 kg (20 to 25 lb.) gain is considered healthy. For a twin pregnancy, the recommended weight gain is 16 to 20 kg (35 to 45 lb.). Note: Short women should use the lower end of the range of weight gain.

How does your weight gain all add up?

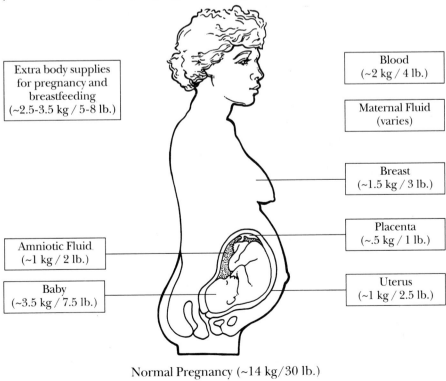

Extra body supplies for pregnancy and breastfeeding (~2.5-3.5 kg / 5-8 lb.)

Amniotic Fluid (~1 kg / 2 lb.)

Baby (~3.5 kg / 7.5 lb.)

Blood (~2 kg / 4 lb.)

Maternal Fluid (varies)

Breast (~1.5 kg / 3 lb.)

Placenta (~.5 kg / 1 lb.)

Uterus (~1 kg / 2.5 lb.)

Normal Pregnancy (~14 kg/30 lb.)

CHAPMAN

Do I need a vitamin/mineral supplement while I'm pregnant?

Nutritionist: If you follow the "Food Guide for Pregnancy and Breastfeeding" on p. 16, the only supplement you may need is iron. Meeting the high iron requirements of the second and third trimesters from food alone can be a challenge, so supplements are useful. Talk to your doctor about your need for supplements. Also, get to know the iron-rich foods listed on p. 18. The lists of other food sources of folacin, calcium, and fiber on p. 18 can also help you make the best food choices for your baby.

What can I drink when I'm pregnant?

Nutritionist: Water, juice, milk, and soup are good choices. Try to have 1.5 litres (6 cups) of fluid daily. No safe level of alcohol intake during pregnancy is known; so it is best to avoid alcohol completely. Remember — beer, cider, wine, coolers, and hard liquor all contain alcohol. Too much caffeine can have adverse effects on pregnancy. Limit yourself to two mugs of coffee or four cups of tea per day. (See p. 26 for more information about caffeine and alcohol and

some alternatives to caffeine-containing and alcoholic drinks.)

I find it hard to drink much milk. How can I get three to four servings daily?

Nutritionist: Choose cheese and yogurt for some of your servings. However, vitamin D is not found in cheese or yogurt, so it is important to have some fluid milk or skim milk powder daily.

Try these ideas:
- eat cereal with milk for breakfast,
- eat cream soup made with milk,
- mix milk half-and-half with coffee for café au lait,
- blend milk with fruit and yogurt for a quick breakfast shake,
- add skim milk powder to hot cereal, cocoa, mashed potatoes, canned soup, and casseroles, or
- sprinkle Parmesan cheese on salads and casseroles.

What about pesticides on fresh vegetables and fruit?

Nutritionist: It's safe to eat fresh, washed vegetables and fruit. The nutritional benefits more than outweigh the very small risk of pesticide residues. If you are concerned about pesticide residues, you can minimize your exposure to them by washing vegetables and fruit well and peeling where appropriate. It is also a good idea to choose locally grown foods and a variety of produce.

I'm busy — how can I prepare healthy, well-balanced meals quickly?

Nutritionist: Here are some ideas for when your time and energy are running low!
- Plan ahead for those busy times.
- Make a grocery list so you'll need to shop only once a week.
- Cook larger quantities so you can freeze a meal for another day.
- Keep meals simple when time is tight.
- See the following list of "baby-building foods" for menu ideas.
- Enjoy healthy meals when you eat out. Even some fast-food outlets feature salads and healthy ethnic choices such as burritos and chili. Choose milk or juice instead of pop, and pack some

fruit for dessert.
- Travel with convenient snacks to nibble on throughout the day. Keep dried fruit, granola bars, crackers, and fruit juice packs in your purse, office drawer, or car.

Does eating well during pregnancy have to cost a lot?

Nutritionist: Healthy foods don't have to be expensive — look for the best buys from each food group.
- Grains: bread, rice, pasta, and cooked cereal
- Vegetables and Fruit: potatoes, turnip, squash, cabbage, carrots, sweet potatoes, frozen peas, and corn; frozen juice concentrate, canned fruit, apples, bananas, and fruit in season
- Milk Group: skim milk powder, canned milk, and cheese slices
- Meat Group: peanut butter, split peas, lentils, baked beans, eggs, sardines, and ground beef

For suggestions on ways to eat well and save money on food, check with a nutritionist at your local health unit/ department.

How about a list of some of the best "baby-building foods" for meal and snack ideas?

Nutritionist: Here are some smart choices, loaded with the best for your baby. Enjoy these "baby-building foods":
- milk;
- yogurt with added fruit;
- raw broccoli or cauliflower with yogurt dip;
- lentil soup;
- split pea soup;
- salmon, liverwurst, or peanut butter sandwiches on whole-wheat bread;
- fresh orange or cantaloupe;
- orange juice;
- bran muffin and cheese;
- whole-grain cereal topped with raisins and milk;
- trail mix made with dried fruit, nuts, and seeds;
- or bean-and-cheese-filled tortillas.

For help with other food-related concerns, such as vegetarian eating, food allergies, or food safety during pregnancy, consult a nutritionist at your local health unit/department.

Physical Activity throughout Pregnancy

Keeping Active

Physical activity is an important part of everyday life. It can help with the stress of pregnancy, help your body's recovery after the baby is born, and help you feel good. Keeping active throughout this time may also minimize or help prevent some problems like backache, varicose veins, constipation, and excessive weight gain.

Talk to your doctor before starting or continuing your activity program. The type and amount of exercise you do during pregnancy must match your personal level of fitness, medical history, the stage of your pregnancy, and any other points specific to you. Physical activity, kept within reasonable bounds (which have not as yet been strictly defined), is not usually harmful to mother or fetus. The following safety tips will give you general guidelines to follow throughout your pregnancy and may help you with an active-living lifestyle.

General Safety Guidelines

- Listen to the signals your body sends you. *If it hurts* — don't do it! Pain is your natural built-in warning signal telling you to stop the activity immediately. Talk to your doctor if you feel any pain or discomfort. Also stop if you are feeling tired.
- Doing *something* is better than doing nothing. Sitting up takes more energy than lying down; standing takes more energy than sitting; moving around takes more energy than just standing; and walking takes more energy than just standing and moving around.
- Keep your heart rate under 140 beats per minute when exercising. Exercise at a comfortable pace — use the talk test (you should be able to talk comfortably during exercise). If strenuous activity is performed, do not exceed 15 minutes in duration.
- Exercising in hot, humid weather or getting overheated, could injure your

baby. (Your internal temperature must not exceed 38.7°C / 101.7°F.)
- Drink liquids before, during, and after exercise to replace lost fluids.
- Avoid jerking, jumping, jarring, bouncing movements and any activity with sudden stops and starts. Wear comfortable, supportive shoes when doing any activity.
- Hormonal changes relax your muscles and connective tissues and make your joints less stable. This will make you more susceptible to strains and sprains. Contact and competitive sports are to be avoided!
- Warm-up before any activity, including stretch activities. Warming-up will release fluid to lubricate your joints in preparation to stretch safely. See the stretching section for more detail.
- After the fourth month, do not exercise while lying on your back. This can cut off the blood supply to the uterus and depress the baby's heart rate. Lay on your side, not on your back.
- Refer to the section "Going Down and Getting Up" for the safety of your back.

Active-Living Lifestyle

Living actively and participating in everyday activities you enjoy is fun. Invite others to join you for a walk, or to join you at the pool for a swim. Take a dog for a walk. Continue your exercise program if you had one before becoming pregnant. Changes may be necessary; consult with your physician. Generally, this is not the time to take up a new exercise program.

Non-weight-bearing, low-intensity aerobic exercises are recommended if you have not been active before pregnancy. They have less risk of injury, especially to the joints.
- Cycling on a stationary bike is preferable to bicycling outdoors because of the changes in balance that may occur during pregnancy.
- Swimming may feel very comfortable because the water supports your weight, and balance problems or clumsiness usually disappear. It also encourages blood flow to the uterus.

- Water aerobics have a support benefit similar to swimming; be cautious of repeatedly landing heavily on your feet on the pool's cement surface.
- Walking is one of the best weight-bearing exercises you can do. A two-minute walk can be taken almost anywhere at any time. Get off the bus two to three blocks early; park further away from where you are going; get up and go for a two-minute walk during TV commercials; walk to lunch three or four blocks away; take the stairs instead of the elevator. If there are many stairs, take the elevator some of the way and climb the rest. This may also help to strengthen your leg muscles.
- Strength training can be cautiously continued for those actively involved before pregnancy. Do not hold your breath at any time during your workout. Avoid heavy lifts. Some common strength-training exercises to avoid are: leg curls in a lying-down position, bent-over rows, dead lifts, vertical rowing on a machine, machine biceps curls if the pad is directly against your abdomen. Strength train with lighter weights and avoid equipment that will put pressure on your abdomen.
- Water skiing is to be avoided because of the potential danger of high-speed falls causing water to forcefully enter the uterus.
- Downhill and cross-country skiing are recommended only with caution and only for the experienced skier. Falling is dangerous. Care must be taken.
- Ice skating is not recommended because falls on the ice may be seriously damaging.
- Low-impact aerobics are recommended for those already participating. Be cautious of bringing your knees up too high, and of large, exaggerated movements.
- Step (bench) aerobics are recommended for those already familiar with this type of workout. You are encouraged to use the platform only, with the minimum amount of height. High kicks and jumping movements are not recommended.

Going Down and Getting Up

Back awareness is important as you adjust to the increasing weight of your advancing pregnancy. The following steps will help to support your back as you move from a standing position to a lying position, or as you pick up something from the floor. Please make sure you get up slowly to prevent dizziness.

Going Down

1. Keep your knees slightly bent (not locked) when standing. This relieves the stress on your lower spine and helps you to balance the weight of your body.

2. Move down onto one knee, placing your hands on the middle of your thigh as you ease yourself down.

3. Take your other knee down and bring yourself onto your hands and knees.

4. Use the weight of your arm to help slide yourself onto your side.

5. Ease your way onto your back, using the strength of your arms to help.

Getting Up

When getting up, reverse the steps you took in order to go down.
1. Use the strength of your arms to bring your body onto your side.
2. Turn yourself over onto your hands and knees.
3. Bring one knee up and place your hands on the middle of your thigh in preparation to push off.
4. Use the strength of your legs and the push-off from your hands on your mid-thigh to bring yourself to a standing position.

Stretching Exercises

Stretching will help reduce muscle tension, and increase range of motion to allow for freer, more flexible movement. Most people are flexible in one area but not in another. What is comfortable and possible for one person is not necessarily so for another. When you are stretching, you will feel a slight pull in the area being stretched. If you feel pain or discomfort, stop or adjust the stretch. Stretching is not meant to be painful.

Stretching Tips
• Breathe regularly.
• Hold the position and stretch for 20 to 60 seconds. The stretch feeling is like a slight, comfortable pull. The extent of the pull will be different for each person and each joint.
• Stretch both sides.
• If it feels uncomfortable or wrong, STOP — Don't do it!

Shoulders and Back Area
Stand away from the wall with your knees slightly bent, and feet hip width apart. Stretch your arms up with your hands against the wall (you are not pushing the wall, just placing your

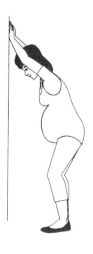

arms in this position). Tilt pelvis inward. Relax your neck, and keep it in alignment with your body. Some people feel this stretch in the arms as well.

Shoulders and Chest Area
Stand sideways against or close to the wall. Place feet hip width apart and parallel to the wall, or at whatever width feels most comfortable to you. Bend your knees slightly and tilt hips inward. Bring your arm up to approximately shoulder height, with your palm against the wall. Again, you are holding your arm in this position, not pushing against the wall (adjust the height of your arm to your own comfort level). Repeat with the other arm.

Lower Leg Area
Extend one leg behind you, keeping your body in alignment (align your spine with your back leg and square your hips off so they are facing the wall). Face feet towards the wall, not rotated in an outward or inward direction. Remember, you are not pushing against the wall; you are balancing your body for support to position yourself comfortably for the stretch. Repeat with the other leg.

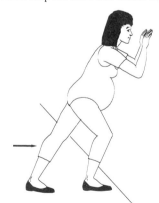

Upper Leg Area
You can use a chair, sofa, low table, desk, or any other structure that is stable (the height of what you use will depend on how tall and how flexible you are). Place one leg behind you so your foot is rested on the chair and your knee is pointed

to the floor. Bend the knee of your supporting leg (the one you are standing on) slightly to support your lower back. Tilt your hips in (pelvic tilt). If you need more of a stretch, change the angle of your hips to tilt inward more or rest your foot on a higher structure. Repeat with the other leg. This stretch can also be done by holding your foot behind you with your hand; however, stay close to something you can hold on to in case you lose your balance.

Back of the Leg (Hamstring Stretch)

Sit on a table, desk, couch, or bench, or anywhere you can stretch your leg out to a fully extended position. Keep your back straight and bend forward slightly from your lower spine area. Relax your head and your arms. Remember, this stretch is for the back of the leg only (do not try to reach your feet by extending your hands or try to put your head toward your knees). Repeat with the other leg.

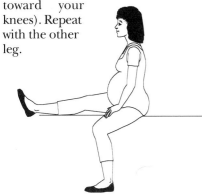

Back

This exercise will help to relieve the pressure of the enlarged uterus on your spine. Kneel on your hands and knees (use the directions in the "Going Down and Getting Up" section to get into posi-

tion). Keep your back flat, do not collapse your spine or let it sag down. Keep your head and neck in alignment with your spine. Round your back up and at the same time tighten your abdominal and buttock muscles (drop your head to follow the alignment of your neck). Slowly relax and allow your back to return to the flat position. Repeat to your own comfort level up to a maximum of 10 to 15 times.

Strengthening Exercises

Your muscles need to be prepared for the birth of your baby. They need to be worked and strengthened in the following areas.

Kegel Exercises

Kegel exercises strengthen the vaginal and perineal area for birth and for after the birth. This exercise can be done anytime, anywhere — standing, seated, or lying down (after the fourth month, lying flat on your back is not recommended). Tighten the muscles around your vagina and anus (these are the muscles used to stop the passing of urine). Hold the contraction for as long as is comfortable, then relax. Increase the time to eight to ten seconds and repeat the exercise throughout the day (work up to approximately 25 times per day). Do not hold your breath while you are contracting your muscles, keep breathing normally.

Squatting

Squatting is sometimes used as a position of comfort during labour and as a

birthing position. You will use many muscles to hold yourself in this position and even to get into the position. Therefore, your muscles need to be exercised.

If you have knee or joint problems do not attempt to do this exercise. Position your back against the wall to help yourself down into the squatting position with your feet away from the wall and a little wider than hip width apart. Keep your feet flat on the floor. Do not extend your knees over your toes; keep your knees over your heels as you go down below parallel, bringing your buttocks close to the floor (this need not be uncomfortable; position yourself at a level you are able to hold for 30 to 60 seconds). To get out of the squat position, use your hands and arms to help yourself right down onto the floor so you're sitting down. Use the directions given in the "Going Down and Getting Up" section to return to a standing position.

Wall Push-Ups

Stand facing the wall. Place your hands approximately shoulder width and height against the wall. Keep your back straight, your hips tilted in (pelvic tilt), and your knees slightly bent. Bend your elbows to bring yourself closer to the wall (inhale as you do this). Exhale as you extend your arms to push yourself away from the wall. This exercise will help to strengthen the backs of your arms and you may also feel your back muscles working. Only do as many as you are comfortable with.

Thigh Stretching and Strengthening

During birth, your legs may be apart for long periods of time. Stretching your inner thighs will help prepare your muscles for this. Sit with your legs apart (you may be more comfortable sitting against a wall) and the bottoms of your feet together (knees out). Place your hands under your knees and gently press both knees towards the floor — do not push with your hands. Hold that position for 10 to 20 seconds and then relax. Remember to keep breathing normally throughout this exercise. Do not hold your breath.

Then, press both knees towards the floor while providing resistance with your hands under your knees. Hold for 10 to 20 seconds and then relax. Do not hold your breath.

Abdominal Exercises to Strengthen Stomach Muscles

Stomach Muscle Separation

As the uterus expands during pregnancy, the abdominal muscles bear most of the pressure. They form the strong but elastic "wall" behind which the baby can grow safely. In some pregnant women, the tissue that helps keep these muscles tight softens and weakens, causing a noticeable muscle separation down the middle of the stomach. Before starting an activity program, it is important to check for this separation and to talk to your doctor about any width of gap in order to prevent any problems. Until the gap is closed, exercises that rotate the trunk, twist the hips, or bend the trunk to one side should be avoided. More strenuous stomach muscle exercise should also be left until later.

To check for separation, lie on your back with your knees bent and feet flat on the floor. Lift your head about 20 cm (8 in.) off the floor, keeping your chin tucked in. Place your hand flat along the middle of your stomach (fingers pointed towards toes) and measure the number of finger widths between the bands of stomach muscle (do not poke your fingers into the gap).

Stomach Muscle Tightening

Lying on your back with knees bent, breathe out while pulling in your abdominal muscles and pressing the curve of your lower back into the floor. Relax and breathe in. Repeat to your own comfort level to a maximum of eight to ten times.

Modified Curl-Ups

Lie flat on your back with knees bent and arms hugging your abdominal area so that they support the stomach muscles. Breathe in, then slowly raise your shoulders slightly off the floor (do not strain) while breathing out, and push your lower back into the floor. Stop short of where a bulge would be caused between separated stomach muscles. Hold this position for two normal breaths, then slowly lower your head to the floor and relax. Repeat six to ten times or however many times are comfortable for you. This exercise can be done every day if it feels comfortable for you.

Alcohol and Other Drugs

Alcohol and Pregnancy

No one knows for sure how little or how much alcohol can harm a developing baby. The most important thing to remember about drinking alcohol while pregnant is that when you drink, so does your baby. Alcohol can affect the baby's fast-growing tissues, either by killing cells or by slowing their growth. The baby's brain is most severely affected by alcohol.

Wine, coolers, cider, beer, and hard liquor all contain alcohol. If you have already consumed small amounts of alcohol during your pregnancy, be reassured that the risk of damage to your baby is low. However, it would be best to stop drinking for the rest of your pregnancy. If you drink regularly, or "binge" (drink heavily on occasion), you increase your chances of having a healthy baby by stopping immediately.

Children born to women who drink while pregnant may have physical and mental birth defects that vary in severity. In severe cases, these babies are said to have Fetal Alcohol Syndrome: they are smaller than normal and tend to have facial, joint, and limb abnormalities. They may also have heart defects, poor co-ordination, and mental retardation. Other potential problems include behavioural difficulties such as hyperactivity, extreme nervousness, and poor attention span. These effects are lifelong, yet they can be prevented by avoiding alcohol during pregnancy.

There is no known safe level of alcohol use during pregnancy. To be safe, a woman should stop drinking alcohol entirely while pregnant. Women who find this difficult to do on their own should consider contacting their local health unit/department or alcohol and drug clinic for assistance. Self-help programs such as Alcoholics Anonymous can also provide support and understanding. Al-Anon is a useful self-help group for family members. For more information on self-help programs, see the article "A Guide to Further Resources" at the back of this handbook.

Smoking and Pregnancy

The effects of smoking on your health and that of your baby are most severe if you yourself smoke. However, inhaling second-hand smoke may have similar (although less severe) health effects on you and your baby. The effects appear to increase with the amount of smoke inhaled, either directly or as a result of exposure to someone else's smoking. The more you smoke, the more likely you are to experience problems with the placenta, with bleeding early or late in pregnancy, with premature and prolonged rupture of the membranes, and with preterm delivery. Scientific evidence also links smoking to miscarriage and low infant birth weight.

As far as your baby is concerned, tobacco smoke reduces the supply of oxygen and constricts the blood vessels. This results in slower growth and development during the critical time before birth. As a result, the child's physical and mental development can lag behind those of other children the same age. This developmental lag can last until the early teenage years and even later. There is also early research evidence to suggest that the children of parents who smoke have an increased risk of developing cancer. Certainly, those children tend to have more chest infections and hospitalizations during their first year of life.

Self-help programs for pregnant women and their partners are offered by the Canadian Cancer Society. The Society can also provide signs for offices, cars, and homes, so parents can let others know that these areas are smoke-free. If you want to designate a room in your home as a smoking area, this area should be well ventilated to the outside. It should not be used by the pregnant mother or by any children in the home.

CHAPMAN

Books on how to quit smoking can be obtained from your local bookstore. If you prefer to have group support for quitting, many communities offer classes. You can find out about them by contacting your local health unit/department, the Canadian Lung Association, the Canadian Cancer Society, and/or smokers' information and treatment centres listed in the Yellow Pages of the telephone directory. For more information on self-help programs and group support, see the article "A Guide to Further Resources" at the back of this handbook.

Are Any Drugs Safe during Pregnancy?

There are some drugs that, after many years of use during pregnancy, have shown no evidence to suggest that they may be harmful to the unborn child. Other drugs are not known to be either safe or unsafe. Still other drugs are known to be extremely harmful, resulting in problems such as withdrawal symptoms in the newborn baby, complications in later infant life, and physical and emotional problems that may last into the infant's adult life. Consult your doctor for further information about any drugs you are wondering about.

If you have an illness during your pregnancy, your doctor may prescribe medication, choosing one that is the least likely to be harmful to your baby. If you are planning a pregnancy or are already pregnant, you should review with your doctor all of the drugs you and/or your partner may have been using, including prescription drugs, over-the-counter drugs, or street drugs. Don't stop using your prescription drugs without consulting your doctor.

For women who use street drugs, change in drug use requires time and support. The first step is to consult your doctor, who can assist you with your withdrawal and recovery process. Alcohol and drug treatment centres and detox centres can help you and your unborn baby undergo a safe withdrawal and begin necessary treatment.

If you or your partner have used or presently use intravenous drugs, there are some additional risks you need to be aware of, particularly concerning AIDS and hepatitis B. Discuss present or previous use of intravenous drugs with your doctor or a public health nurse.

Some Drugs Deserve Special Comment

- Caffeine, one of the most widely consumed "drugs," may cause problems. Many of us take caffeine without realizing it, since it is found not only in coffee, but in ordinary tea, chocolate, cola beverages, and several over-the-counter drugs as well. It is known that caffeine enters the baby's circulation and that the baby's system is unable to process it. There are concerns that caffeine in large amounts may be harmful, so it is a good idea to limit your daily intake to two mugs of coffee or four cups of tea. Better yet, avoid these drinks altogether. Choose alternatives such as fruit juices, grain-based non-alcoholic beverages, herbal teas (rose-hip, mint, lemon balm, raspberry leaf), milk, or water with a slice of lime or lemon.
- If you drink herbal teas and are using them frequently, discuss the variety used with your doctor and/or someone knowledgeable in herbal medicines since there may be concern with some pregnancies.
- Marijuana contains tar. When smoked, it produces carbon monoxide, which has the same effects as smoking cigarettes. There is also evidence of other harm to the baby and mother, so marijuana should be avoided.
- More severe in producing harmful effects on the baby are narcotics such as heroin, methadone, tranquillizers, and other mood-altering drugs. A baby who has shared such drugs with its mother during pregnancy is at risk. The baby will require special treatment to reduce the effects that may appear immediately after birth, after a few days, or much later.
- Cocaine is a powerful, addictive drug that increases the risk of the placenta separating from the uterus, lower birth weight, and preterm labour. If a pregnant woman has used or is using cocaine, she should discuss this with her doctor. Withdrawal from cocaine should be medically supervised.

Self-help programs such as Narcotics Anonymous and Cocaine Anonymous can provide understanding and support. For more information, see the article "A Guide to Further Resources" at the back of this handbook.

Once again, to be safe, you should not take medications of any kind, except on the instructions of your doctor. Although the likelihood of harm to the baby diminishes after the first 12 weeks, doctors try to avoid prescribing medication at any time during pregnancy to prevent unnecessary risk to the developing fetus. When drugs are needed, follow your doctor's instructions. Some drugs react with other drugs and become dangerous to the baby when taken together; therefore, be sure to talk to your doctor about *all* the drugs you are taking.

Saunas/ Hot Tubs/ Hot Baths:
Approach with Caution

Saunas, hot tubs, and hot baths can be very relaxing. It is important, however, not to let yourself become too hot while pregnant. If you want to use a sauna or hot tub/bath, do not stay in longer than ten minutes. Also, make sure to lower the temperature to below 38.9°C or 102°F. Have another adult around to help you get in and out. If you feel dizzy or faint or have a rapid pulse, irregular heartbeat, stomach pain, or tingling in the feet or hands, you should get out immediately. Again, make sure you have help.

De-Stressing Tips

We hear a lot about stress these days. Bookstores are bursting with books on the subject. Businesses are conducting stress-reduction programs for their employees. You can even buy audio tapes to improve your stress-coping skills. Everyone is at least trying to do something about it. And for good reason.

In simpler times, stress was less of a problem. When we were in direct combat with nature, struggling to survive, our stress-alarm system was a necessity. It helped us fight or run away when faced with danger. But in today's world, the dangers are more subtle and more complex. Many different things can cause stress in our lives. And for many of these things, immediate action is often impossible. This means that we have to squelch our "fight-or-flight" response many times throughout the course of a day. Years of denying this response takes its toll on our bodies.

As a part of everyday living, stress affects us physically and emotionally. It is associated with happy as well as unhappy situations. Life changes bring stress. When too many changes are occurring at the same time, illness may result. As pregnancy is a time of many changes, you can be sure there is already some stress in your life (as is normal and healthy). But if you find your stress levels rising too high for comfort, consider the following ideas.

1. Talk about your worries with someone you trust — your doctor or nurse, a supportive friend, and/or a family member.

2. Try to make sure you have time to yourself every day. Otherwise, you may feel pulled in all directions at once and be unable to enjoy your pregnancy or think about your baby. Give yourself a "free day" every once in a while, to read, swim, bathe, walk, or just stay in bed if you want to.

3. Take the time for daily physical activity such as walking, yoga, or swimming. Even simple stretching will help you.

4. Make a point of doing relaxation exercises every day (see the relaxation tips in the article "Rehearsing for Labour" on p. 51).

5. A sudden stress such as the death of a loved one, a move away from a familiar place, or the loss of a job may cause you to feel depressed, tired, or hopeless. These feelings are natural and probably healthy, as well; however, if they persist, you should seek professional help.

6. Take an easy-going approach, which often helps to reduce stress and irritants. Think about different ways to handle situations.

7. Meet your worries head on. Are you unsure about whether to go back to work? Find out about your job rights and unemployment insurance. Does your partner seem distant? Talk things over and try to clear the air. Whatever your concern, taking action will make you feel better and help you solve your problem.

8. Take the time to sit down and think things through calmly, to arrive at decisions. If your job involves a lot of responsibility, set goals and figure out how to meet them. Then set up daily plans and schedules for projects.

9. Plan ahead whenever possible. Make the necessary arrangements at work so you can leave your job with everything in good order. Prepare your other children for the arrival of the baby. Make sure you have help around the house in the first few weeks after the baby is born.

10. Sign up for stress-management classes, if available.

Travel

Deciding whether to travel during pregnancy depends on how you feel and how difficult the journey is. It is not a good idea to travel if you're ill, fatigued, or prone to dizzy spells.

It is all right to drive a car to do errands and so on, as long as you are comfortable sitting behind the wheel. Seatbelt regulations do not exclude pregnant women, so you must wear a seat belt. Extensions are available if the seat belt is too short. The lap belt must be worn low and fit snugly across the upper thighs, not over the abdomen. The shoulder belt should also be worn (see below).

If you are travelling short distances by bus and have a flexible schedule, you will be more comfortable if you avoid peak travel times.

Longer trips, on the other hand, will probably require planning to make sure the journey is safe and comfortable. The following suggestions can help you plan.

• Consult with your doctor ahead of time, especially in the first and last three months of pregnancy.

• On long car trips, pre-plan a rest stop every 160 km (100 miles) to accommodate your need to use the bathroom frequently. Take a short walk during rest stops and bring along a snack.

• Wherever possible, drive on the major, more frequented roads and have someone accompany you.

• Consider train or air travel as an alternative to travelling by car. You might find such travel less tiring.

• Keep in mind that, if you want to travel in the last month of pregnancy, most airlines require a letter of clearance from your doctor.

• Before buying an airline ticket, find out about the airline's policies regarding travelling when pregnant, in order to avoid any problems with travel arrangements.

• If you are travelling to a country where immunization or other measures to prevent illness are required, you should check with your doctor or local health unit/department.

CHAPMAN

And What about Sex?

"Since I became pregnant, I'm just not interested in sex any more.... Jack says he understands, but I can tell he feels hurt."

"Craig seems really put off sex now that I'm pregnant. The problem is, I want to make love more than ever, and it's getting to be a real problem between us! ... He's afraid he'll cause a miscarriage or hurt the baby or something!"

Few subjects stir up more emotion or cause more confusion and miscommunication than sex, especially when it comes to sex during pregnancy and after childbirth. Needless to say, either expecting that nothing will change or abstaining totally from sexual intercourse may make both partners unhappy and frustrated. Fortunately, there is a middle ground. It is possible for a couple going through pregnancy and parenthood to maintain an intimate relationship, provided the partners are both willing to make it a priority, and an enjoyable one at that!

One of the major stumbling blocks to sexual intercourse during pregnancy is the belief that having sex will hurt the baby, risk miscarriage, or cause premature birth. The truth is that, in most cases, sexual intercourse can continue until very late in the pregnancy, if the couple so chooses. Conditions such as history of miscarriage, vaginal bleeding, pain, or loss of fluid from the uterus may affect sexual relations. All of these conditions should be brought to the doctor's attention. However, as Dr. R.W.D. Stevenson, of Vancouver's Shaughnessy Hospital Sex Medicine Unit, points out, "Even if there is a medical indication for limiting sexual activity, it usually means sexual intercourse only. There are a variety of ways to give and receive pleasure that may or may not lead specifically to orgasm for both partners, but that will allow ongoing opportunities for intimacy."

Often, however, the reasons for backing away from sexual intimacy during pregnancy are more social or cultural than physical. Historically, there is a taboo in many cultures against sexual activity during pregnancy. Many of us may have unwittingly inherited this taboo. A number of religions in different parts of the world regard the pregnant woman, like the menstruating woman, as being in some way threatening, unclean, or even too sacred for sexual intimacy. In the world of psychiatry, a traditional school of thought views motherhood as asexual. In other words, a woman is biologically designed to separate herself from her sexuality once she becomes a mother so that she can attend to her child. Fortunately, this limited view is being replaced by one that suggests that pregnancy and child rearing can actually enhance a woman's sexuality and make her feel more tuned in to her own body and sensations.

In support of this point of view, Sheila Kitzinger, author of many books on pregnancy and childbirth, encourages women to enjoy lovemaking during pregnancy because it creates feelings of relaxation, happiness, contentment, and luxurious self-satisfaction. These feelings, she says, create the best possible emotional climate in which to prepare for motherhood. Spontaneous, affectionate, and gentle lovemaking, to her way of thinking, creates a relaxed attitude. This attitude helps the expectant mother cope with the inconveniences and discomforts of pregnancy and is excellent preparation for childbirth.

Sexual intercourse during pregnancy does require some adjustments, however. It can be uncomfortable for a pregnant woman to lie on her back. Pillows — lots of them — can be a big help. For example, a woman who gets indigestion or heartburn if she lies flat on her back can place pillows under her head and shoulders. Experimenting with different positions is also a good idea. Side-by-side or sitting positions work very well. When the baby has engaged in the pelvis and there is little extra room, the woman can try lying, crouching, or kneeling with her back to her partner so that he enters her from behind. Being flexible enough to try different ways of making love makes it possible for a couple to enjoy intercourse right up until the woman goes into labour.

What happens, however, if she doesn't want to make love, or doesn't get excited, or can't achieve orgasm? Many couples may find that, at different stages of the pregnancy, the woman feels uninterested in sex. The first trimester, or first three months, is a time of tremendous emotional and physiological adjustment. She may be very tired and suffering from nausea and may view intercourse with distaste. During the third trimester, or last three months, she may very well be worn out from the extra weight she's been carrying around. She may also be suffering from heartburn and lack of sleep, in which case she is unlikely to be eager for sex. Not all women are affected by these changes in the same way — some feel more open, giving, and sensual than ever before!

When it comes to shifts and changes in his partner's sexuality during pregnancy, it is best if the man accepts these changes gracefully, offering her his love and support throughout. And it is important for a woman going through a period of low interest in sexual intercourse to find other ways to show her partner how much she loves him. His need to feel loved may be particularly acute if, as sometimes happens, he feels shut out of her pregnancy, worried about how much the coming baby will interfere with their life together,

CARNES

even jealous of her reproductive powers and ability to carry the baby. She can offer him sympathy, laughter, good food, conversation, affection, stroking, massage, sexual variations — whatever is within her capacity to reassure him of her love.

When it comes to maintaining a love relationship after the baby is born, according to Dr. Stevenson, "The majority of couples find that there are changes, but where they run into difficulty is where they don't anticipate the changes; this leaves them less able to deal constructively with any problems that may occur."

Some of the changes are physical. Women who have had an episiotomy may find intercourse painful until their incision has had a chance to heal. Some women experience vaginal pain because of lower hormone levels, which can cause a decrease in sexual drive, a thinning of the vaginal walls, and a decrease in natural lubrication (which is why a water-soluble lubricant or contraceptive cream may be necessary). Breastfeeding could also cause a reduction in lubrication, although studies indicate that women who breastfeed tend to resume sexual interest and sexual activity earlier than those who do not.

Most doctors advise the new mother to abstain from intercourse for the six weeks it normally takes for her body to return to its pre-pregnancy state. But for many couples, it isn't necessary to wait that long. They may feel very tender towards one another after their baby is born, especially if they've experienced the birth together. Once the discharge from the uterus after delivery (lochia) is no longer red, the episiotomy or perineal tears have healed, and the mother feels comfortable and rested, there is no reason for them not to resume their sexual relationship. In any case, even if sexual intercourse is uncomfortable, a couple can express their sexuality and love for one another in different ways (e.g., touching, stroking, massage, etc.).

There are other factors, however, that might cause difficulties. The new mother may feel a low interest in sex as a result of having her life shaken up. She may be feeling exhausted, having to take care of the new baby, her mate, and possibly other children. After going through the physical changes of having a child, she may feel that her body is no longer attractive. Thus, she may suppress her sexual desires for fear of being rejected. She needs her partner to nurture her, care for her, and reassure her that she is a beautiful and loving person.

The father, on the other hand, may feel that he has been replaced by the new child and is no longer the most important person in his partner's life. He may also feel emotionally drained after the birth. In his role of supporter, however, he may not get any opportunity to express his real feelings or concerns. He may want to express his love for his partner but is afraid that he will hurt her or that she won't have time for him. He needs to remember that his feelings

are appropriate, which means accepting his need for emotional support, encouragement, and reassurance from his partner that her love for the baby has not decreased her love for him.

The first year after the birth of a baby can be a very stressful time for both partners, but it doesn't need to be devastating, according to Dr. Stevenson, "if they talk to one another with the attitude that their bond is strong enough that problems can be resolved, that their partner wants to hear their needs and concerns, that their partner wants to help resolve issues, and that both of them want to work on the relationship." He notes that having both partners participate in prenatal education and the birth process can have a very positive influence on a couple's sexual relationship. "There is a greater sense of sharing and a stronger bond, so that even if there are sexual problems, they are more likely to get through them." It is also important for new parents concerned about their sexual relationship to recognize that they can seek help, whether from their family doctor, public health nurse, or another trusted professional.

In coping with the changes a baby brings, couples may need to call on all the resources of humour, compassion, and understanding they can muster. They may even need to remind themselves, Sheila Kitzinger asserts that "mothers and fathers are also husbands and wives — and lovers — and have a right to their sexual identities." It's all too easy for them to get caught up in the demands of child rearing and career and forget what brought them together in the first place. On this point, Dr. Stevenson deserves the last word: "The whole reason they got together, made the commitment, had the child, and want to go on together is because there was something important and meaningful between them. So they can't take the relationship for granted. They've got to do some maintenance on it."

Baby in Progress

The development from two tiny cells to a fully formed baby is a fascinating story. Below are some of the highlights from that story, from fertilization on.

The First Trimester

The first trimester (or first three months) is a critical time in the baby's life. It's a time of rapid growth and development. It's also a time when the baby is most susceptible to such hazards as smoking, infections, drugs, and X-rays.

Time	Weight & Length	Events
1 day		The sperm and ovum unite.
7 to 10 days	·	The fertilized ovum becomes implanted in the lining of the uterus. The placenta begins to form.
2 weeks	⊖	The embryo is now a layered disc on the uterus wall. The mother misses her menstrual period.
4 weeks	0.4 g (0.01 oz.)	The beginnings of the embryo's eyes, ears, nose, spine, digestive tract, and nervous system are present. The tube for the future heart starts beating.
8 weeks	22-24 mm (1 in.) 1 g (.036 oz.)	The fetus now has all the organs that a full-term baby would have. The heart is functioning. Bone formation begins.
12 weeks	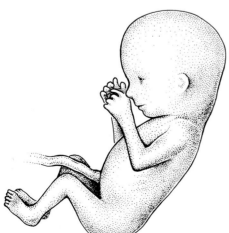 9 cm (3 1/2 in.) 15 g (1/2 oz.)	The baby's sex can be distinguished. "Baby" teeth buds are present. Fingernails and toenails are forming. Immature kidneys secrete urine to the bladder. The fetus can now move in the amniotic fluid, but can't be felt by the mother.

The Second Trimester

During the second trimester, or the second three months of the fetus's life, the brain develops considerably. In fact, most of the brain's development occurs during the period from now until 18 months after birth. During the second trimester, though, the fetus cannot live outside the mother's body because its respiratory and cardiovascular systems are not developed enough.

Time	Weight & Length	Events
16 weeks	16 cm (6 1/2 in.) 100 g (4 oz.)	The face looks more human, the head has hair, and the ears stand out. Between the eighteenth and twentieth weeks, the fetal heart can first be heard with a stethoscope. The baby's movements may be felt by the mother. (The mother may not feel the baby's movements until 18 to 20 weeks, especially with the first pregnancy.)
17 weeks		The baby begins to store some of the mother's antibodies, which slowly increase until birth.
20 weeks	25 cm (10 in.) 300 g (10 oz.)	Eyebrows and eyelashes appear. A fine downy hair (lanugo) appears all over the baby's body and may still be present at birth. The baby's skin is thin, shiny, and covered with a creamy protective coating called vernix. Oil glands appear. The baby's legs lengthen, and the baby can move its legs well. Teeth develop — enamel and dentine are being deposited (can begin as early as 14 weeks). (By the end of the fifth month, the baby is about half the length of a newborn baby.)

Time	**Weight & Length**	**Events**
24 weeks	30 cm (12 in.) 600 g (1 1/4 lb.)	Sweat glands form. The baby has a lean body. The baby's skin is red and wrinkled. Primitive breathing movements begin. A substance called surfactant is formed in the lungs. This substance helps the lungs to expand normally after the baby is born.

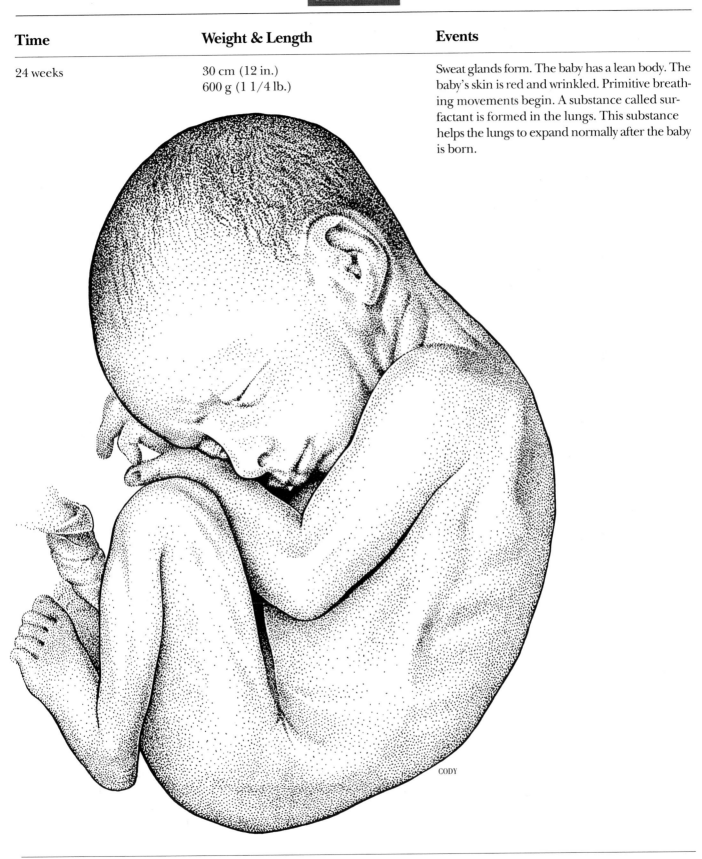

CODY

26 weeks		The baby's outline may be felt through the mother's abdomen. The eyes may be open now.

The Third Trimester

During the third trimester, or the last three months of pregnancy, the baby could survive if delivered before full term, but would need special care. The closer to full term, the more ready the baby is to cope with the birth process and to exchange the shelter of the uterus for life in the outside world.

Time	Weight & Length	Events
28 weeks	35-37 cm (14 in.) 1100 g (2 lb. 5 oz.)	The baby's body is still lean, but the skin is less wrinkled and red. The baby can now store iron, calcium, and other nutrients.
32 weeks	40-42 cm (16 in.) 1800-2100 g (4 lb.-4 lb. 7 oz.)	The baby's skin is pink and smooths out as the fat forms under it. The baby develops a sense of taste. The baby becomes aware of sounds outside the mother's body. The male baby's testicles begin descent into the scrotum. The pupils in the baby's eyes can react to light.
36 weeks	45-47 cm (18 in.) 2200-2900 g (4 lb. 11 oz.-6 lb. 5 oz.)	The baby's body is rounded and usually plump. The downy hair on the baby's body begins to disappear. The baby's blood has a high concentration of hemoglobin (this may occur as early as 28 weeks). The baby's skin is smooth, pink, and covered with a greyish-white cheeselike substance (vernix). The baby continues to increase the store of maternal antibodies and, thus, resist some diseases.
40 weeks	45-55 cm (18-22 in.) 3200 g + (7 lb. +)	Head hair is usually present. The testes of male babies are now in the scrotum, and the labia majora of female babies are now developed.

The baby is now full term — a new chapter in the baby's story is about to begin!

Staying Comfortable during Pregnancy

Pregnancy affects every system of your body — your reproductive, respiratory, digestive, cardiovascular, nervous, and urinary systems. With all of this activity going on, no wonder you feel uncomfortable from time to time! The following chart lists some of the common discomforts of pregnancy and describes what can be done about them. Every woman's pregnancy is different, so you will probably not experience many of these discomforts; but whatever type of discomfort you do experience, there are steps you can take to make yourself more comfortable.

Week	What can happen	What you can do
1 - 4	*Absence of menstruation (Amenorrhea):* Hormonal changes stop the menstrual cycle so that the uterine wall lining will build up to cushion and feed the baby.	
5	*Tingling and tension in breasts:* Hormones cause changes in breast tissue to prepare them for nursing.	
	Fatigue: The energy demands of pregnancy are greater than before. The mother tires much more easily.	• Fatigue is an important sign from your body that you *need* extra rest. • Become aware of your limitations and alternate periods of activity and rest, making sure to stop before becoming overtired. • Eat small, well-balanced meals several times a day and drink plenty of fluids (also see p. 19).
	Increased frequency of urination: The uterus presses on the bladder, decreasing its capacity.	• To limit the need to urinate at night, restrict the amount of caffeine-containing beverages (coffee, tea, etc.) taken in the evening.
	"Morning sickness" (nausea and vomiting): This is caused by hormonal action, tension, and/or fatigue. The condition usually lasts about 8 to 12 weeks only, but may persist longer. It can occur any time of the day.	• Eat smaller amounts of food every one to two hours throughout the day (include some protein) rather than three large meals. • Try eating unsalted crackers or dry toast as a snack before getting out of bed in the morning; it may also help if you get out of bed slowly. • Avoid fatty and fried foods. • Drink fluids such as clear tea, apple juice, and ginger-ale. • Try eating cold meals to avoid nausea triggered by food odours. • Avoid drinking liquids with meals. • Be sure there is fresh air in the bedroom while resting, and in the kitchen while cooking. • Wear loose clothing, especially around the chest and waist. • Brush teeth or rinse mouth after vomiting to protect teeth from the dissolving action of stomach acids. • Notify the doctor if vomiting persists and you become concerned.
	Headache: Your body goes through physical and emotional changes during pregnancy, which may cause headaches.	• Eat small, well-balanced meals several times a day. • Drink plenty of liquids.

Week	What can happen	What you can do
	Headache: (continued)	• Try to avoid caffeine, cigarette smoke, stuffy rooms, fluorescent lights, activities that cause eye strain, etc. • Get adequate sleep at night and rest during the day. • Ask someone to massage your neck, shoulders, face, and scalp. • Get plenty of fresh air. • Apply a cool or warm washcloth (whichever works best) to your forehead and the back of your neck. • Avoid taking any pain medications unless discussed with your doctor.
6	*Increased vaginal secretions (thin and milky):* These are due to hormonal changes and increased congestion.	• Wear small pads, underwear with cotton gussets, and looser slacks. • Shower or bathe frequently. • Keep the area clean and dry. • Contact your doctor if there is itchiness, or frothy, smelly, or coloured discharge, as this may indicate a mild infection.
	Self-concern and sleepiness: The cause is thought to be hormonal (part of natural protection for mother and baby). You may not feel as active as usual.	• Realize that this is normal. • Take it easy. • Take time to relate to the baby growing in the womb.
	Enlargement of breasts and darkening of the brown part (areola): Continued changes occur in breast tissue in preparation for breastfeeding.	• Wear a good supporting bra for comfort. • Wear a light bra for sleeping if your breasts are really heavy.
6 - 9	*Light-headedness:* The circulatory system is working harder and may adapt slowly to standing or sitting.	• Get up or change position slowly. • Maintain good posture and exercise regularly. • Avoid skipping meals.
	Shortness of breath: Body chemistry changes, requiring increased breathing.	• Realize that this is usually normal. • Check with your doctor if there is a history of heart problems in your family.
12 or after	*Appearance of small lumps on the areola (called Montgomery's tubercles):* These lumps contain fatty substances that lubricate the areola.	• Recognize that these changes are normal.
	Appearance of a brownish "tan" on your face called chloasma (mask of pregnancy) or a line running from the navel to the pubic area (darkening of the linea nigra).	• Know that these signs will occur in some women and that the mask disappears after the baby is born (the linea nigra may remain).
13 or after	*Little nausea, less bladder pressure, less fatigue:* The uterus rising up in the abdomen takes pressure off your pelvic organs. Your body is now more adjusted to the state of pregnancy.	• Be aware that the chances of having a miscarriage or spontaneous abortion are very small at this stage. • Enjoy pregnancy.
16 or after	*Secretion of breast fluid* (may begin anytime from now until birth)*:* This water-protein matter (colostrum) comes before breast milk.	• Recognize that this is normal.
16 - 22	*Quickening:* The baby's movement is felt by the mother. This may occur earlier or later than noted here.	• Recognize that the sensation (e.g., bubbling, fluttering, knocking) can differ for each pregnancy. • Note the date, and tell the doctor on the next visit; this is a useful milestone by which to date the expected birth.

Week	What can happen	What you can do
20 - 21	*Low back pain:* This is often due to the stretching of the ligaments attaching the uterus to the pelvis, an increase in the size of the abdomen, resulting in poor posture, and normal softening of the pelvic joints.	• The key to short-term relief is to pull in your stomach muscles, tighten your buttocks, and tuck in your seat, thus flattening your lower back; this is called the pelvic tilt exercise; try the pelvic tilt on all fours, and the shoulders and back stretch as well (see the article "Physical Activity throughout Pregnancy" on p. 22). • Sit in straight-backed chairs whenever possible. • Wear shoes with lower heels; running shoes and crepe-soled shoes are very comfortable. • Sleep on your left side, with your legs spread as though running; ensure that the mattress is firm and there is a pillow under the knee of the right leg for support. • Maintain good posture. • Try heat and massage or apply cold, whichever decreases the pain. • When lifting objects, bend from your knees, not with your back. Avoid heavy lifting.
	Throbbing of legs and appearance of varicose veins: Pressure in the abdomen sometimes causes pooling of blood in leg veins. If you have a history of varicose veins, you may find them worse during pregnancy.	• Elevate your legs when lying down by arranging a support for their full length; let your knees bend slightly to allow your legs and feet to roll out naturally; make sure that your legs are higher than your heart, but at an angle no greater than 45°. • Walk to help the circulation in your legs. • Wear support hose if recommended by your doctor; avoid knee-highs and garters. • Use a foot rest when sitting. • Contact the doctor.
	Hard, dry bowel movements (constipation): Early in pregnancy, this can be a result of changing food habits or hormone action that slows bowel activity; later, it may be caused by enlargement of the uterus, which displaces the intestines and compresses the colon. Iron supplements can also cause constipation.	• Chew your food thoroughly. • Drink plenty of fluids (six to eight glasses per day); a glass of warm water before breakfast may also prove helpful. • Eat whole grains and plenty of vegetables and fruit, including dried fruit (especially prunes), to keep stools soft. • Exercise regularly (e.g., walking, swimming). • Put your feet up on a foot stool when using the toilet, so that the thighs provide support and comfort for the abdomen. • Go to the bathroom when you feel the urge; do not hold back, but don't force the bowel movement. • Relax and take time for your bowel movements. • Do not use suppositories, laxatives, or enemas unless recommended by your doctor.
	Mild swelling of ankles, feet, hands, and face: This is caused by extra fluid that remains in the tissue due to hormonal changes, increased blood volume, and the pressure of the growing baby.	• Elevate your legs and feet whenever possible. • Avoid lying on your back. • Try lying on your left side when resting or at night; this may help decrease pressure on major veins and allow blood to flow back to the heart more easily. • Avoid wearing clothes or accessories that are constricting (e.g., watches, rings, or knee socks with elastic tops). • Do exercises that will stimulate the flow of blood from the legs to the heart, such as walking, swimming, or rocking in a chair. • Talk to your doctor.

Week	What can happen	What you can do
25 and after	*Upper back pain:* This is due to the enlarging uterus.	• Sit tall, using pillows for comfort. • Have someone give you a massage. • Stretch shoulders and back area (see "Physical Activity throughout Pregnancy" on p. 22).
30 and after	*Appearance of purple or red marks (striae) on abdomen and breasts:* This is due to stretching of the skin and increased activity of hormones from the adrenal cortex, which may cause itchiness.	• Massage your skin with lotion or oil to alleviate the itching. • Avoid moisturizing or perfumed creams, which could cause a rash.
	Increased fatigue: This is due to new demands made by the fetus and your body.	• Maintain an adequate diet. • Have frequent rest periods. • Know your personal limitations. • Try to rest *before* getting tired.
	Braxton Hicks contractions: Irregular, painless contractions of the uterus may be noticeable now.	• Inform your doctor if the contractions are regular and become uncomfortable.
	Muscle cramps in legs, especially at night: This is thought to be due to pressure on abdominal nerves, fatigue, and/or calcium phosphorus imbalance.	• Make sure you get enough calcium in your diet or talk to your doctor; he or she may advise a calcium supplement. • Avoid fatigue. • Elevate your feet. • Exercise daily. • Take a warm bath before going to bed. • Stretch your lower leg area before going to bed (see "Physical Activity throughout Pregnancy" on p. 22). • Press your foot against a firm surface to relieve foot cramps. • Lie down, straighten your legs, and use your foot muscles to push your heel out and pull your toes in (towards the nose). • Lie down, straighten your legs, and have someone gently push back on the sole of your foot; meanwhile, press the sole of your foot against your partner's hand, keeping your leg straight and your toes pointing upward.
35	*Awkwardness and some depression:* You may feel impatience at the seeming endlessness of pregnancy and frustration with the limitations imposed.	• Remember, it will not be long before the baby is born. • Talk things over with a friend, especially one who has had a baby and understands.
36	*Heartburn, gas (flatulence), and constipation:* This is due to the pressure of the uterus on the stomach and intestines, as well as hormonal action.	• Eat a mildly acidic food such as yogurt or buttermilk. • Eat small, frequent meals instead of large meals. • Avoid fried, fatty, and highly spiced foods. • Drink plenty of liquids, but avoid drinking with the main meals. • Elevate your head and shoulders while resting. • Do not bend or lie down immediately after a meal. • Avoid using baking soda. • Avoid coffee and cigarette smoke. • Try a leisurely walk or sitting quietly and breathing deeply.
	Hemorrhoids: These are due to pressure interfering with circulation in the veins; they are aggravated by constipation.	• Exercise daily. • Do pelvic floor (Kegel) exercises (see "Physical Activity throughout Pregnancy" on p. 23). • Elevate your legs and buttocks when lying down; do not lie flat on your back.

Week	What can happen	What you can do
	Hemorrhoids: (continued)	• Avoid sitting or standing for long periods. • Keep bowel movements soft to avoid straining.
	Sudden groin pain: This is due to sudden stretching of ligaments that support the uterus. It may occur with abrupt movements such as sneezing, coughing, or standing up quickly.	• Avoid sudden movement. • Bend slightly at the hips if expecting to cough or sneeze.
	Shortness of breath: The top of the uterus is now pressing against the diaphragm, decreasing lung capacity. This is more troublesome when you are attempting to lie down. It can be aggravated by smoking and insufficient iron in your diet, which causes anemia.	• Maintain good posture. • Ventilate rooms well and breathe fresh air. • Try taking deep, slow breaths through the mouth. • Stretch shoulders and back area (see "Physical Activity throughout Pregnancy" on p. 22). • Elevate the head of your bed or prop your head and shoulders to assume a semi-sitting position for sleeping. • Get plenty of rest and avoid over-exertion. • Wear loose clothing, especially around the chest and stomach. • Always stand up straight to allow plenty of room for your lungs to expand.
	Difficulty sleeping: As pregnancy progresses, your increased size may make it difficult to sleep in your normal position. The baby's kicking or increased bladder pressure may keep you awake during the night.	• Before going to bed try: a warm relaxing bath; a snack with a warm drink (avoid eating a big meal and beverages containing caffeine); using extra pillows for support; a massage; deep breathing; relaxation exercises — including self-hypnosis, meditation, and visualization (see the article "Rehearsing for Labour" on p. 51). • Try to maintain a regular sleep routine. • Exercise daily.
	Stuffy nose and allergies: Sometimes a stuffy nose and allergies occur during pregnancy, even among women who have not had them before.	• Avoid smoking or being in a smoke-filled room. • Try to determine what it is you are allergic to. • Place warm, moist towels on your face. • Breathe steam from a hot shower, a pot of boiling water, or a vaporizer. A cool mist humidifier may also help. • Massage your sinuses (rub on the bony ridge above and under your eyebrows, under your eyes, and down the sides of your nose). • Drink extra fluids. • Try salt-water nose drops (made from one-fourth teaspoon of salt dissolved in one cup of warm water). • Do not use antihistamines unless recommended by your doctor.
37 - 38	*Improved breathing — decreased abdominal distention:* With the first pregnancy, "lightening" may have occurred. It feels as if the baby dropped! The uterus settles down in the pelvic cavity. With subsequent pregnancies, lightening may not occur until labour starts.	• Tell the doctor when this happens.
	Increased frequency of urination: The uterus is again pressing on the bladder, decreasing its capacity.	• Do pelvic floor (Kegel) exercises (see "Physical Activity throughout Pregnancy" on p. 23).
3 - 4 days before labour	*An increase in Braxton Hicks contractions*	• Avoid becoming involved in strenuous activities. • Conserve energy. • Complete packing for the hospital. • Make last-minute household arrangements.

Your Changing State of Mind

CHAPMAN

You may discover or have already discovered that the nine months of pregnancy are not just a time of physical change. They are also an emotional preparation for the demands of parenthood. Yet because every woman's personality and situation are so individual, it can be even harder to predict the kinds of emotional changes you might experience than to predict what kinds of physical changes you might go through. The important thing to remember is that however alarming your mood and personality changes might seem, they are in many cases normal and temporary. Usually they are caused as much by the hormonal changes going on in your body as anything else. By openly discussing your feelings (with your partner, your doctor, a close friend or relative, and/or your public health nurse), you can usually clarify misunderstandings and get rid of unnecessary fears. You may also find that the progressing pregnancy brings with it a great many positive emotions and gives you a fresh perspective.

The First Trimester

During the first trimester of the pregnancy (i.e., the first three months), your outlook may be coloured by your personal situation:

- Is this a planned pregnancy?
- Are you a single mother?
- Are you (and/or your partner) employed?
- How will the pregnancy affect your career?
- Will finances be a problem?
- Is your relationship with your partner a good one?
- Are you feeling too young or too old to deal with the changes a baby will bring?

The emotional reactions to being pregnant may range from great joy to feelings of doubt and sadness. On the other hand, the pregnancy may seem unreal. It may be some time before you can accept the fact that you really are pregnant.

At this stage, it is quite natural to wonder whether your baby will be healthy and whether you will be able to cope with (additional) children. It is also natural to wonder whether you will be able to handle the possible pain of childbirth, and whether you are prepared for parenthood. It is quite normal to experience sudden and unexpected mood changes, with bouts of crying or laughing. Thoughts and fantasies may come to mind that you have never thought about previously. You may need extra attention and affection and feel very dependent upon others. Maybe, too, you will feel very irritable and self-centred at times. If so, keep in mind that it is not a self-indulgence to spend time thinking on your own, developing greater self-awareness. To help focus your thoughts, take a look at the article "What Kind of Parent Will I Make?" on p. 47. Talk over your thoughts and ideas with your partner and/or support persons.

The Second Trimester

If your pregnancy seemed at all unreal during the first trimester, the reality will become more immediate during the second trimester. You will undoubtedly feel, if you have not before, that you really are going to have a baby. There is the thrill of feeling the baby move and hearing the baby's heartbeat (ask your doctor to let you and your partner hear this). The baby may become more interesting to you, and you might begin to imagine what he or she is like. Former worries may not disappear completely; however, you may find that you are less preoccupied with them.

The Third Trimester

As the pregnancy progresses, you may start feeling anxiety about the birth, and you may begin wanting it to be over with. If anxiety about birth and labour becomes a source of stress, you may need to concentrate more on the relaxation and breathing techniques that are an important part of preparing for labour (see the article "Rehearsing for Labour" on p. 51). Both you and your baby will benefit from staying calm, as undue stress can prolong labour. The "nesting instincts" that many mothers experience at this time may also help you focus on your preparations for labour, birth, and the new baby. Mingled with a sense of impatience may be times of unexpected joy.

Knowing that the emotional ups and downs of pregnancy are part of the experience of becoming a mother does not always make them easier to deal with.

Certainly, the support of those close to you can help you through even the most difficult times. But pregnancy can be a time of vulnerability. Although the care with which you look after yourself can help ensure that you give birth safely to a healthy baby, a small number of parents must face the difficult experience of losing a baby (through a miscarriage, ectopic pregnancy, stillbirth, or other misfortune following birth). If this happens, the emotions of grief, guilt, or despair can be very difficult to deal with. In such situations, knowing where to turn for outside support can be important. Your doctor can help with information and possibly counselling or referral. Help is also available from the hospital social worker and nurses, the public health nurse, and others who have been in similar circumstances.

Another problem that some women face during the vulnerable time of pregnancy is hostility from a husband or partner. A partner who has been physically or verbally abusive in the past may be more so once you become pregnant. This is sometimes caused by increased strain on the relationship or feelings of jealousy and resentment towards the baby. Even though you may have tolerated a degree of physical and verbal abuse before becoming pregnant, you must seek help if faced with this situation now. It is not just you who are at risk, but also your baby. Talk to your doctor and public health nurse. The difficult emotions of pregnancy often are made more difficult by family violence. A local crisis centre can also provide help. For more information, see the article "A Guide to Further Resources" at the back of this handbook.

Cause for Concern?

Thanks to modern medical know-how, difficulties can often be anticipated and appropriate care taken in advance of the baby's birth. You owe it to yourself and your baby to tell your doctor about any concerns you may have during your pregnancy, regardless of how small or insignificant you may think these concerns are. This is especially important if you experience any of the following:
- any illness or fever (don't take any medication, unless your doctor recommends it),
- any exposure to rubella (also known as German measles),
- itchiness or rashes of any kind,
- sudden, unusual thirst,
- persistent coughing,
- excessive fatigue,
- dizziness, headaches, dimming and/or blurring of vision,
- sudden or severe swelling of your feet, hands, or face,
- sudden weight gain,
- frequent vomiting,
- abdominal pain or rigidity,
- bleeding from your vagina, bowel, or bladder,
- a burning sensation when urinating,
- coloured, frothy and/or foul-smelling vaginal discharge, or vaginal discharge causing itchiness or irritation,
- a gush or trickle of water from your vagina,
- persistent negative feelings about your pregnancy and care of the baby,
- depression or periods of weeping that don't go away,
- family medical conditions such as hereditary diseases, diabetes, high blood pressure, and kidney disease, or
- noticeable change in the baby's movements over a 24-hour period.

If any of the above apply to you, contact your doctor right away!

Feeding Your Baby — Making the Decision to Breastfeed

Canadian mothers are breastfeeding in increasing numbers. Making the decision to breastfeed is easy for some women because they were breastfed. Their friends and relatives have breastfed successfully and can give them support. Their partners understand how important breastfeeding is to the baby's health and growth.

Although breastfeeding is a natural process, it is learned and it does take commitment and support. One way to get support is to talk about breastfeeding with the important people in your life before the baby arrives.

For some women the decision is harder because they're not sure they can breastfeed. Perhaps friends and relatives are not able to provide information. Their partners may be unsure about the benefits of breastfeeding and concerned about relationship changes. Breastfeeding away from home may be a concern, as is returning to work.

Seek advice from someone in your community who has breastfed, or phone your local public health nurse who can talk to you about breastfeeding and give you the number of the local La Leche League representative or other community supports.

Breastfeeding has many benefits. Breastfed babies have fewer allergies and illnesses. Breastfeeding is easy and takes less time than bottlefeeding (after the first few weeks once you and your baby have learned how). Breastfeeding costs less ($20/month for food for you versus $90-150/month for formula). Breast milk is easy to digest, has exactly the right nutrition for your baby, and adjusts to your baby's changing needs.

Note: Working mothers can continue to breastfeed (see "Working Outside the Home" on p. 45).

Breastfeeding is the best way to feed babies. The Canadian Pediatric Society recommends that babies be given only breast milk until they are four to six months old and that breastfeeding go on into the second year of life.

What to Do During Pregnancy to Prepare for Breastfeeding

- Check your breasts by your sixth month of pregnancy (your doctor will help you). Breasts come in different sizes and shapes. Babies can feed on most breasts. If you have concerns about the shape of your nipples or breasts, discuss your concerns with your doctor.
- Attend prenatal classes and ask about positioning for breastfeeding.
- Get used to handling your breasts so you'll feel comfortable when you feed your baby.
- Buy brassieres that provide comfortable support and are not too tight (usually two sizes larger than your normal fit).
- Continue to eat well from the "Food Guide for Pregnancy and Breastfeeding" on p. 16. You will make milk regardless of what you eat; but, by eating well, you will have more energy to look after yourself and your family. See "What Should I Eat When I'm Breastfeeding?" on p. 71.
- Attend a meeting of La Leche League or another group of breastfeeding mothers.
- Ask about rooming-in practices in the hospital where you plan to deliver your baby.

Getting a Good Start to Breastfeeding in the Hospital

- Put your baby to the breast as soon as possible in the first hour or two after birth.

BURGESS

DECOSTE

CARNES

• **LOOK** at the commercial formulas on the market. Make sure you know which ones are suitable for newborns and what they cost. Discuss formula types with your doctor.

• **PLAN** ahead in your budget for the monthly cost of formula. Compare powdered, concentrate, and ready-to-serve (which is much more expensive). You can't know exactly how much your baby will want, but you can use an average of 960 mL (32 oz.) per day to estimate what you need to buy.

• **PLAN** ahead in your budget for buying nipples and plastic or glass bottles that can be cleaned easily. Some of the novelty shapes are hard to clean. Bottles with disposable liners are more expensive.

• **READ** the article "Bottlefeeding Your Baby" on p. 87.

If you choose not to breastfeed and can't afford commercial formula **do not give your baby regular cow's or goat's milk or soy milk during the first nine months.** Talk to your public health nurse or nutritionist about other options.

• Ask that your baby receive no food or drink other than breast milk.

• Breastfeed when your baby is hungry (on demand). Let your baby guide you — it could be as often as every hour.

• "Room in" to have your baby with you 24 hours a day.

• Ask about breastfeeding support in your community.

Three Important Breastfeeding Words to Know

• **Positioning:** How you hold your baby so that you can be comfortable and your baby's mouth can gather in your areola and nipple.

• **Latching:** Bringing your baby and the breast together so your baby can suckle and get the milk out of the breast and into his or her mouth. Use of pacifiers (soothers) during the first six to eight weeks may interfere with your baby's learning to latch on to the breast.

• **Let Down:** The prickly, rushing feeling that tells you that the milk in your breast is there for the baby to drink. Some women have milk and don't feel this.

Are there women who can't or shouldn't breastfeed?

Yes, there are rare medical conditions and necessary drug treatments that prevent breastfeeding or make it unwise. Talk to your doctor if you are concerned.

What if you choose not to breastfeed, or are one of the few people who can't?

Breastfeeding is the feeding of choice. The next best thing to breastfeeding is commercial infant formula.

How Will I Know My Baby is Breastfeeding Well?

You can hear your baby swallowing during feeding.

Your breasts are full before feedings and soft after feedings.

By three or four days of age your baby will:

• have at least four or five wet diapers (look or feel wet) in 24 hours,

• have urine that is pale and odourless,

• have at least two or three bowel movements in 24 hours,

• have bowel movement colour anywhere from brownish to seedy mustard and yellow,

• have bowel movements at least the size of a "loonie,"

• breastfeed at least eight times in 24 hours,

• be content after most feedings.

Put this information in a handy location now so you can refer to it as soon as you are home with your baby!

Working Outside the Home

Maternity Benefits and Paternal Leave

Up-to-date information on maternity benefits, including benefits for the father, are available from the Unemployment Insurance Commission. Check the blue pages of the telephone directory under Government of Canada, "Employment and Immigration Canada." Some private plans and company policies also provide benefits. Ask your employer. (For more information, see the article "Legal and Practical Issues" on p. 49.)

What You *Do* at Work

Is your job very tiring or stressful? Is it physically hard (including lifting, pushing, pulling, stretching, climbing, or balancing; sitting or standing a long time without breaks)? Do you work long hours? Are you exposed to infection or dangerous chemicals and fumes? Do you get overheated (see article on p. 21)? If you answered yes, talk to your doctor about the risk to you and your baby during pregnancy and breastfeeding. Talk to your supervisor about possible job changes during this time.

If you stand for long periods of time, shift your weight from one foot to the other and/or put one foot up on a footrest. If you sit a long time, change positions and use a footrest, box, or book under your feet. Have two breaks

CHAPMAN

45

or rest periods each day. When you have a break try to find a quiet spot, a chair to put your feet up on or a couch to lie down on.

Getting to and from work during the rush hours can be tiring when you are pregnant or a new mother. Some women have changed their schedules to avoid rush hour. Can you?

What You Eat

Fit eating into your busy working day, both before and after baby's birth. Start the day with food and something to drink. Use break times to rest and have a snack and drink. Some breastfeeding mothers try to have a snack or something to drink around the time they're pumping milk to save for their babies.

Check for more information and ideas in: Canada's Food Guide to Healthy Eating (available from your Health Unit), "Food Guide for Pregnancy and Breastfeeding" (see p. 16), and "What Should I Eat When I'm Breastfeeding?" (see p. 71).

Whether you are pregnant or a new mom, take care of yourself. Eat a variety of foods and enough food to give you the energy you need.

Breastfeeding and Working

You can successfully breastfeed and work outside the home. If possible, make your return-to-work plans flexible. You may find that having a baby alters your plans. Many women who breastfeed find it easier to start back to work part time.

Most working moms who breastfeed successfully know other women who are also successful breastfeeders. Get to know other women who work and breastfeed successfully and who can give you support. Read books about working and breastfeeding: *The Working Woman's Guide to Breastfeeding*, by Anne Price and Nancy B. Dana, and *Bestfeeding: Getting Breastfeeding Right for You* by Mary Renfrew, Chloe Fisher, and Suzanne Arms.

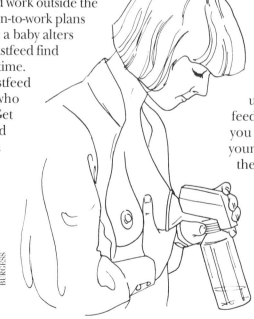

- Get a good start on breastfeeding before you return to work (see "Learning How to Breastfeed" on p. 69). Remember that the first few weeks are the most important for establishing successful breastfeeding. You and your baby need to find out what works for the two of you.
- Contact your public health nurse, La Leche League or breastfeeding support group, and/or a lactation consultant for help and information.
- Talk to your supervisor before returning to work. Discuss the importance of support for breastfeeding at work to you and your baby's health. This means a quiet, smoke-free place to feed or express milk; access to a fridge to store expressed milk; flexible work hours; a reasonable workload.
- Learn how to express your milk by hand or pump. Start storing milk ten days to two weeks before you expect to return to work (see "Expressing and Storing Breast Milk" on p. 86).
- Introduce a bottle or cup to the baby before you return to work. If your baby won't take it from you, get help from your partner or another support person.
- Make a list of things to take to work, such as tasty and nutritious snacks (see p. 71), bra pads, breast pump (if needed), emergency phone numbers of support people, clean cup or sterile jars, plastic freezer bags or disposable liners to store breast milk. Expressed milk needs to be kept cool. If you don't have a fridge at work, check with your public health nurse for ways to store your milk.
- Make sure that your child care provider understands the importance of breastfeeding to you and your baby. Discuss when you will be gone; when you will breastfeed your baby; when, what, and how you expect the caregiver to feed your baby. Talk about supplies, such as frozen breast milk or formula. Make sure your caregiver knows how to prepare and store bottles safely.

Remember: When you breastfeed and work, extra rest helps and is worth planning for!

DECOSTE

What Kind of Parent Will I Make?

Once you become a parent, you will probably learn things about yourself that you never knew before; and if you share the tasks of parenting with a partner, the two of you will undoubtedly learn things about each other that you might never have learned otherwise. Although it is impossible to be completely prepared for parenthood, it might help to think about how you would handle some of the challenges of one of the most important roles you will play in your lifetime.

Knowing what you expect of yourself and of others may make it easier to deal with some of the parenting decisions you will be called on to make. Discussing your views with your partner will allow you to see where you agree and where you might disagree. Two parents need not always agree on how to raise children; however, after a thorough discussion, you should at least reach some sort of compromise. Young children who have the love, attention, and security they need soon learn the differences in their parents' methods and react accordingly, just as they will have to do with different people throughout their lives.

The following are subjects to think about and discuss with your partner and/or support persons:

- roles with respect to household chores now and after the baby is born,
- thoughts about what parenting means to you,
- your reasons for having children,
- what you hope for and expect from your child,
- views on parenting courses,
- the values you wish to teach your children,
- views on mothers who work outside the home, day care, and fathers as caregivers,
- your thoughts on expressing or venting feelings of frustration and/or anger,
- your thoughts on ways to cope with increased demands on your time and energy and feelings of fatigue, and
- thoughts on what you can offer your child.

Think about the following situations. How will you decide to handle them?

- You are not sure how soon your newborn should sleep in a separate room from you.
- Your baby continues to cry, even after being fed and changed.
- Your two-year-old continues to wake twice every night.
- Your young children want to play together, but frequently end up fighting with one another; they are especially difficult to deal with since the new baby arrived.
- One of your children is prone to temper tantrums in public places (e.g., the grocery store).
- You want to go to a party with your friends, but you can't afford a babysitter.

There are many good books available that provide information and guidance on the subject of child raising. As well, you can speak to your local public health nurse about the various parenting groups operating in your community.

47

Sibling Jealousy: Talk and Teach

Baby Sara is crying. You walk into her bedroom just in time to see Scottie, your three-year-old, trying to take her doll away from her. You're furious and you tell Scottie to apologize for being mean to his baby sister. "Sorry," says Scottie, looking as if he doesn't mean it. Exasperated, you send him to his room. He bursts into tears and says he wishes you'd send Sara back to the hospital.

A typical scenario? Very. But given enough attention and reassurance that you love him just as much as you do his sister, Scottie will recover from his jealousy. A certain amount of jealousy is to be expected. After all, before Sara came along, Scottie didn't have to share your attention with her. And it can be hard to take a back seat to a baby when you're used to being number one!

Older siblings may react at different times and ages with baby-like behaviour, direct aggression, or maturity and independence. Some jealousy is to be expected, especially if your child is as young as Scottie. You can minimize jealous feelings by being sensitive to the older child's feelings. It helps to prepare the older child for the baby's arrival, in advance.

CHAPMAN

48

As soon as your pregnancy is confirmed, casually talk about it with your older child(ren). Arrange visits with friends or relatives who have small babies. And answer any questions about pregnancy and birth as honestly and simply as you can. There are many books available to help you. (For example, *Where Do Babies Come From?* and *Before You Were Born* by Margaret Sheffield and Sheila Bewley answer a child's questions about birth in a gentle, loving, and direct manner. Both are enjoyable and easy to understand.) You might find the following tips useful as well.

- Each child should have some special time with both Mother and Father before and after the baby arrives.
- If your child seems to cling excessively to Mother, Dad could help by giving the bath, handling the bedtime routine, and taking on other child-care tasks.
- If your child is old enough to have a bed, introduce the new bed now rather than waiting until after the baby arrives. Otherwise, it might be upsetting for the crib to be taken away and given to the baby.
- Make sure the older child has contacts outside the home. Nursery school might be a good idea, or regular visits with another child of the same age.
- Teach the child to respect Mother's rest times both during pregnancy and after the baby arrives. During pregnancy, you and your child should rest at the same time.
- Try to include the older child in the preparation plans (e.g., helping set up the crib or shopping for articles for the new baby). Some children enjoy feeling the baby kicking in the womb, others don't.
- Explain in advance who will be looking after the older child(ren) when Mother goes into the hospital. Make sure to plan carefully so there aren't too many changes or disruptions all at once.
- Take the older child to the hospital to see Mother and the new baby if possible, preferably at a time when no other visitors will be around. If you can, spend some time with the older child before introducing the baby.
- If your older child is willing, give some responsibility in the care of the baby (e.g., helping with the baby's clothes or showing the baby to visitors).
- When people come to visit you and the baby at home, make a point of telling them about the older child's accomplishments. This will reassure the child that he or she is still important.
- Obtain a small gift that the new baby can "give" to the older child(ren).

Should you become concerned about persistent difficult behaviour, consult your doctor or public health nurse.

Legal and Practical Issues

The birth of a baby may be a wondrous event, but there is a practical side to it as well. You may already have decided on your favourite boys' and girls' names, and you may already have enough life insurance to give you peace of mind now that you are taking on a dependent. But there are other practical concerns you might want to consider at this time. Below are some common questions parents ask about the legalities of having a baby.

We've heard that now that we're expecting a baby, having a will is more important than ever. Why is that?

The main reason is that, if either or both of you die, you will want to make sure that your wishes with respect to the care of your child will be carried out. This involves taking a careful look at your friends and relatives. Think about who would be the best person (people) to be your child's guardian(s). Then, after getting their consent, you can make an appointment with your lawyer and either make a will or change your existing will.

Am I entitled to take time off from work?

Provisions vary from province to province. For example, under the British Columbia *Employment Standards Act*, employees are entitled to a leave of absence from work, without pay, so that they can spend time with a new child. A natural mother is entitled to 18 weeks of unpaid maternity leave. This leave period may be extended by up to six weeks if the doctor certifies that it is required. As of March 22, 1991, the Act also provides for 12 consecutive weeks of parental leave for both mothers and new fathers, including adopting parents. An individual is entitled to take parental leave if he or she is:

- the natural mother of a newborn child (total maternity and parental leave may not exceed 32 weeks),
- the natural father of a newborn child, or
- an adopting parent.

To qualify for this maternity or parental leave, an employer must be given at least four weeks' written notice of the day you want to start your leave and a medical certificate or letter from the adoption agency. If both maternity and parental leave will be taken, separate notice is required for each leave.

In British Columbia, there is no minimum period to be completed for an employer before an employee can apply for parental or maternity leave. The employer must keep the job or a comparable position open for the employee after leave ends. Employee benefits (e.g., medical coverage) continue during the unpaid leave period, provided that the employee continues to pay his or her share of any premiums.

To find out what the rules are where you live, contact the Ministry of Labour in your province.

When can I take parental leave?

Again, in British Columbia, both the mother and father may apply for parental leave. Leave may be taken at the same time or at different times. For the natural mother, parental leave must begin when maternity leave expires, unless the employee and employer agree otherwise. For the natural father, leave must be taken within 52 weeks of the child's date of birth. For adopting parents, leave must be taken within 52 weeks of the date the child comes into actual custody.

If the newborn or adopted child suffers from a physical, psychological, or emotional condition and will be at least six months of age before coming into the new parents' actual care and custody, parents are entitled to an additional period of parental leave of up to five weeks. The family's doctor, or the agency that placed the child, must certify that such an additional period of parental leave is required. Total maternity and parental leave may not exceed 32 weeks.

For more information on any provincial rules, call the Employment Standards Branch, Ministry of Labour, listed in the blue pages in the provincial section of your telephone directory.

How soon do I have to register the birth of my baby?

The birth of every child must be registered, usually within 30 days. The completion of the birth registration is the responsibility of the parents. Birth registration packages are often distributed at hospitals. In the birth registration package, you will find the appropriate forms, which must be completed and returned to your provincial registrar. A postage-paid envelope is often provided for this purpose. If your baby was not born in a hospital, contact your provincial registrar's office. (Look under "Birth Certificate" in the provincial section of the blue pages of your telephone directory.)

The doctor who attended your baby's birth will provide a notice of birth to the registrar following the delivery, but it is up to you to complete the registration.

What do I have to do to get a birth certificate for my child?

A birth certificate is necessary for entry into the school system, obtaining a passport, immigration, and other purposes. If your baby was born in the hospital, the hospital staff will provide you with an application form for the birth certificate (the application is included in the birth registration package). If your baby was not born in a hospital, contact your provincial registrar (look under "Birth Certificate" or "Vital Statistics" in the provincial section of the blue pages of your telephone directory). A birth certificate cannot be issued until your child's birth is legally registered.

Can we give our baby any last name we like?

If both parents sign the Registration of Birth, the surname may be any chosen name as long as both parents agree.

When only one parent signs the Registration of Birth, the surname may also be any chosen name. Under these circumstances, however, there is a requirement that the particulars of the parent not signing the form not be included. The parent signing the form must also complete a Statutory Declaration to establish why the other parent has not signed the certification section of the Registration of Birth. This Statutory Declaration is located on the reverse side of the registration form.

Remember that your child must have a given name (first name) and a surname (family name) in order for the birth to be legally registered. Middle names are optional. Hyphenated or combined surnames are acceptable, but cannot have more than one hyphen.

How do I arrange for Family Allowance?

After your baby's birth has been registered, you can apply for Family Allowance. The application for Family Allowance is a separate form from Registration of Birth and is often available at the hospital. If you do not receive the form at the hospital, you can call the Health and Welfare Client Services Centre, listed under "Family Allowance" in the blue pages of your telephone book.

Does my baby get medical services coverage automatically?

No, one of the parents will have to take responsibility for registering your baby as a dependant on your family medical coverage. If your family pays premiums directly to the health insurance plan, the hospital will provide you with the necessary forms and information.

If medical coverage is provided through an employer or union, you will have to contact them. If you are covered through the social services ministry, you must contact your social worker to obtain medical coverage for your baby.

Rehearsing for Labour

Just as every pregnancy is unique, so is every labour. There is no "one sure way" to breathe, relax, and get comfortable during labour. This article presents some relaxation techniques and breathing patterns that you can use, separately or in combination, to:

- cope with pain by reducing your stress levels,
- work with your contractions so you can help with your baby's birth,
- ensure an adequate supply of oxygen to your body and your baby's,
- conserve energy and prevent yourself from becoming needlessly tired, and
- deal with feelings of fear, anxiety, or anger.

You will want to practise the various breathing and relaxation techniques during pregnancy to determine which work best for you. Becoming familiar with all of the techniques is a good idea, as it is not until labour is in progress that you will know which will be the most helpful to you. If possible, practise the techniques with the person who will be with you during the birth. Your birth companion will be able to:

- help you with the relaxation procedures, and with the various comfort positions you choose,
- signal the beginning and ending of the simulated contractions,
- help you stay relaxed by touching, massaging, talking, breathing with you, and reminding you to move around, and
- give you support and encouragement (see the article "A Guide for Birth Companions" on p. 56).

Relaxation

By learning to relax, you can reduce unnecessary muscle tension. Since labour can be made longer by the release of stress hormones, it is important that you learn to relax your mind and your body. It is helpful to learn relaxation routines with the encouragement and support of your partner, but it is equally important that you be able to relax by yourself. To start, quiet and pleasant surroundings will be necessary; however, as you develop skills, you will be able to relax even in busy, noisy places.

Try some or all of the relaxation procedures suggested here two or three times a day. You can try them after your prenatal exercises, at bedtime, or when you're feeling upset or tired. Before beginning, you may want to create a peaceful environment with music, loosen your clothing, remove your shoes, and lie on your left side on a firm surface or propped up in an easy chair with pillows. You could also take a deep breath in and out, or even yawn.

Focal Point Concentration/Visualization

Being able to redirect your attention away from an immediate cause of stress or tension can play an important part in helping you relax. During labour, you may find it helpful to focus your attention by looking at somebody or something in the room, thinking about an especially pleasant and soothing memory, or picturing the baby and the surrounding muscles of the uterus working together to open the cervix. When practising your breathing and relaxation before birth, you can try different focal points to see which you prefer. You may wish to have more than one focal point for concentration during labour. Here are some thoughts you can try using:

- floating like a leaf on the ocean,
- resting on a cloud, watching the sky change colour,
- being limp as a rag doll,
- being light as a feather,
- being loose as a piece of cooked spaghetti, or
- melting like butter.

Massage

One of the most useful comfort measures during pregnancy and labour is massage — a smooth, rhythmic stroking or rubbing of a part of the body, such as the face, neck, shoulders, back, thighs, feet, or hands. You can do it yourself, or have a partner give you a massage.

Massage can also be used in combination with another relaxation technique such as touch relaxation (relaxing the various muscle groups in response to a partner's touch). During labour contractions, some women like their partner or birth companion to hold a hand over the tensed set of muscles until they relax. Others prefer firm pressure, which is gradually released as the muscles relax. Still others like to feel gentle massage stroking outward and away from the centre of tension.

There are three basic types of massage.
- **Effleurage** is light, rhythmic stroking of your abdomen. It can be done with two hands making circles on your abdomen, or with only one hand moving back and forth over your lower abdomen, "stroking the baby's head." Corn starch, talcum powder, or hand lotion can be used to make the hands glide more easily. This type of massage can be particularly relaxing during the late stages of pregnancy and can help relieve abdominal pain during labour.
- **Kneading** involves squeezing and releasing a body part — the face, neck, shoulders, back, thighs, feet, and/or hands (what most people think of when they think of massage).

MASSE

• **Counterpressure** involves pressing with the hand on the lower back, to relieve backache. Your birth companion must push with considerable force, holding your hip-bone with the other hand to keep from pushing you over. This type of massage is particularly effective in helping to relieve the type of back pain that can occur during labour.

Touch Relaxation

Touch relaxation is a pleasant and effective relaxation technique that can be very useful during labour. In touch relaxation, the pregnant woman responds to another person's touch by relaxing or releasing tense muscles.

   If you want to learn this technique, here is what you do.
1. Enlist the co-operation of your partner or a friend. Ideally, it should be the person who will be helping you with the birth.
2. Arrange for a quiet time when there won't be any interruptions. You might want to dim the lights of the room, if possible, and put on your favourite relaxing music.
3. Lie on a mattress on the floor. Avoid lying on your back if possible. Ask your partner to kneel beside you in a position that will allow him or her to reach your body easily. Your partner may want to use supporting cushions in order to be as comfortable as possible.
4. Follow the steps in the chart on the next page. Practise the sequence more than once, with your partner trying different types of hand pressure:
   • **still touch:** holding hands in place until there is a release of tension
   • **firm pressure:** pressing the tense area firmly, gradually releasing pressure as you relax

• **massage:** kneading the tense muscles, or stroking the tense area in one direction, away from the centre of your body.

Complete Relaxation

Try to tense and relax each part of your body in turn, using moderate tension, for a period of three to five seconds (tensing too strongly could cause muscle cramps). Breathe in as you tense and out as you relax. Concentrate on how good it feels each time you relax.

Curl your toes tightly...Relax
Pull your toes to your nose (to tense your calves) .....Relax
Harden your thigh..Relax
Squeeze your buttocks together..................................Relax
Pull In your stomach ....Relax
Tighten your chest...Relax
Shrug Up your shoulders...Relax
Flex your arms ....Relax
Ball your hands into a fist ....Relax
Frown or Grimace ....Relax

To end, inhale and begin to tense at your feet, working the tension up through your entire body (feet, legs, abdomen, chest, arms, neck, and head, all in sequence). Hold the tension for three to five seconds. Then exhale and release. Practise this procedure until you achieve a "sinking" or "floating" sensation. It is helpful for you to recognize and remember the feeling of total relaxation so that you can achieve this feeling between contractions without going through the complete routine. Remember to TENSE when breathing IN and RELAX when breathing OUT.

TOUCH RELAXATION

Body part	Pregnant woman	Partner
Scalp	Raise eyebrows.	Using both hands, stroke from the centre of the forehead outward.
Face	Frown.	Place fingers or palm of hand on the side of the head at the temples, press firmly, and release pressure outward.
Neck	Tense neck muscles.	Gently massage back of neck.
Shoulders	Raise shoulders towards ears.	Touch, press, or massage shoulders.
Upper Back	Press shoulder blades towards each other.	Stroke shoulder blades from the centre outward.
Arms	Make a fist and tighten arms, one at a time.	Stroke down the arm from the shoulder to the hand.
Abdomen	Tighten abdominal muscles.	Stroke the lower curve of the abdomen from the centre outward.
Lower Back	Tighten or arch lower back.	Touch, press, or massage the small of the back from the centre outward.
Buttocks	Squeeze buttocks.	Stroke buttocks from tailbone towards the hips.
Legs	Tighten leg muscles, one leg at a time (avoid pointing toes).	Stroke legs upward from foot to hip to promote circulation if legs and feet are swollen.

As a variation, you can try achieving total relaxation simply by concentrating on releasing the tension from each body part in sequence. Initially, relaxing from the toes upward may be easiest, but the sequence can be reversed.

Checking for Relaxation

If you are rehearsing your relaxation with a partner or your birth companion, he or she can check for relaxation by feeling that the various parts of your body are limp and that you look calm and relaxed, maybe even sleepy. When one of your arms or legs is lifted slowly by your partner, it should feel floppy and heavy — neither helping nor resisting the gentle support.

Perineal Massage

Perineal massage is a method used to stretch the opening of the vagina and to decrease the chance of a tear or episiotomy (an incision made in the perineum to enlarge the opening of the vagina). Massage can decrease resistance during the birth. During perineal massage, a woman can locate her pelvic floor muscles and learn to relax them. The use of a water-soluble jelly (e.g. KY) or pure vegetable oil while doing the procedure may soften the tissues. Massage can be started around the thirty-fourth week of pregnancy by the woman or her partner, depending on how comfortable each is with the procedure. For details on how to perform perineal massage, talk to your health care provider or prenatal class instructor.

Breathing

The main purpose of using learned breathing patterns during labour is to maintain a good supply of oxygen to the baby and uterus. Try the following breathing patterns so when the time comes you will be able to use them. Just as your body has adapted to the growing baby and uterus throughout your pregnancy, so your body will be the best guide to the most effective breathing during labour. When practising the breathing patterns suggested here, remember that during labour you will want to:

- concentrate on relaxation as you breathe,
- match your breathing pattern to the intensity of your contractions,
- always start and end each contraction with a deep, relaxed breath, and
- breathe in a slow and relaxed pattern that is comfortable for you.

First Stage Breathing Pattern 1

(approximate length of contraction: 30 to 45 seconds)
1. Take a deep, relaxed breath.
2. Relax from head to toes, relaxing your mouth to relax your pelvic floor.
3. Focus on something in the room, or visualize a favourite image of your own (see the suggestions for "Focal Point Concentration/Visualization" described previously in this article).
4. Use slow deep breathing—in through the nose, slowly out through the mouth, letting your abdomen sink. Your partner should be able to hear you breathing out. Repeat this step six to ten times until the contraction ends.
5. As the contraction ends, take another deep breath.
6. Relax and breathe as usual. You can now move about, change position, and rest until the next contraction, then use slow, deep breathing again.

This slow, deep breathing is useful during the early first stage of labour. It may also be all you need until you reach transition.

First Stage Breathing Pattern 2

(approximate length of contraction: 45 to 60 seconds)
1. Take a deep, relaxed breath.
2. Relax from head to toes, relaxing your mouth.
3. Focus on or visualize your chosen object or image.
4. Use breathing pattern 1 for 15 to 20 seconds of the contraction.
5. Gradually change to shallower breathing—with shoulders and mouth relaxed, breathe in and out through your mouth slowly, moving your chest, but not your stomach.
6. Return to slow, deep breathing.
7. As the contraction ends, take another deep, cleansing breath.
8. Relax and breathe as usual. You can now move about, change position, and rest until the next contraction, at which point you repeat this breathing pattern.

This breathing pattern may be particularly useful during the active first stage of labour.

Transition Stage Breathing Pattern

(approximate length of contraction: 90 to 120 seconds)
1. Take a deep, relaxed breath.
2. Relax from head to toes, relaxing your mouth to relax your pelvic floor.
3. Focus, perhaps on your birth companion's face.
4. Puff in lightly through your mouth, then blow out a longer breath through puckered lips in a pattern comfortable for you (e.g., puff, puff, blow).
5. As the contraction ends, take a relaxed breath.
6. Relax and breathe as usual. You can now move about,

change position, and rest until the next contraction, at which point you repeat this breathing pattern.

Second Stage Breathing Pattern—Birth

(approximate length of contraction: 60 to 90 seconds)
1. Take a deep, relaxed breath.
2. Relax from head to toes, relaxing your mouth to relax your pelvic floor.
3. Focus on the baby coming through the birth canal.
4. Breathe slowly, changing to shallow breathing if necessary for comfort.
5. Take a deep breath in, lean forward, and tighten your abdominal muscles. Relax your pelvic floor and push (but don't push during rehearsal). Hold your breath for five or six seconds, or let the air out slowly with grunts. Allow your body to guide you as to how hard you should push.
6. Release all breath, then breathe in and out comfortably until you get the urge to push again or until you are asked to push.
7. As the contraction ends, slowly sit or lie back and take deep, relaxing breaths.
8. Repeat for the next contraction.

During the second stage of labour, if the baby is being born too quickly, it is sometimes necessary to use panting breaths. The panting helps you control the urge to push. This gives the perineum time to stretch fully and allows the baby's head to come gently. When asked to pant:
1. Put your head back.
2. Breathe in and out lightly and briskly through your mouth.
3. Concentrate on relaxing your pelvic floor and abdominal muscles.

Hyperventilation

As you breathe through the successive contractions in labour, you may suddenly find yourself overbreathing (hyperventilating). This can be caused by any type of rapid breathing when too much carbon dioxide is blown out. The carbon dioxide level in the body regulates the brain in its control of breathing. If you blow out too much carbon dioxide, you may have:
- blurred vision,
- light-headedness or dizziness, which could lead to a blackout or fainting spell, or
- tingling or numbness in your hands and feet, which could progress to cramps or muscle spasms.

If hyperventilation does occur while you are in labour, you can try:
- keeping your breathing shallow (in the upper chest, throat, and mouth),
- slowing down your breathing (especially your exhaling),
- breathing into and out of a paper bag (thus increasing the amount of carbon dioxide you are taking in), or
- holding your breath for a few seconds after a contraction, before exhaling.

What to Take to the Hospital

As you get closer to the big day, you will want to be prepared. The baby obviously isn't going to delay its arrival until your suitcase is packed, so you should have it ready to go well in advance. The things you think you will need during labour should be most accessible. In fact, the items you don't expect to need in labour can be packed separately and left for someone else to bring later on (along with going-home clothes and equipment for you and the baby).

The following list identifies some of the things you might want to put on your packing list. Not all of the items listed below are absolutely necessary. Certainly, none should be considered a prerequisite for giving birth. The articles marked with * are supplied by some hospitals. Your prenatal instructor or birth companion may be able to suggest additional articles.

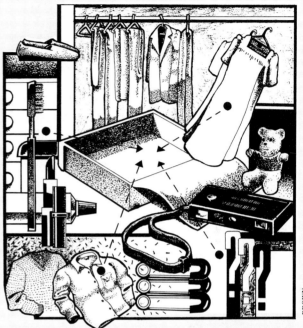

BROWN

Hospital Labour Kit

- *Baby's Best Chance: Parents' Handbook*
- lip balm or lip gloss
- campers' ice (for back pain)
- snack for partner (if the hospital does not provide food in the labour room)
- partner's swimsuit (so he or she can accompany you in the shower)
- camera, flashes, film
- tape recorder (with headphones) and tapes of relaxing music
- personalized focal point (a picture, design, figure, anything you find pleasant to look at)
- sour candies or mints
- breath freshener
- slippers with supportive backs

Grooming Items

cosmetics	dental floss
deodorant	dusting powder
mouthwash	nail file
shampoo	skin lotion*
soap*	shower cap
toothbrush	toothpaste

Clothing

(to be brought in after the baby is born)
- bed jacket or sweater (front-opening for breastfeeding)
- washable dressing gown
- two or three nightgowns* or pairs of pyjamas (front-opening for breastfeeding)
- two or three nursing bras
- panties
- pyjama bottoms or slacks for postnatal exercises
- socks
- sanitary supplies*
- breast pads

Going-home clothes should be packed separately and left for someone else to bring later on, since personal storage in the hospital is usually very limited. Your clothes should be loose-fitting and comfortable. For ease of breastfeeding, you should wear a top that opens in front. Many mothers wear maternity clothes home (not all of the weight gained in pregnancy is lost immediately, so pre-pregnancy clothes may still be rather snug).

Extras

- facial tissues*
- soap for washing underthings
- stationery (pen, stamps, address book)
- announcement cards
- quarters for phone calls

For the Baby

- shirt and gown or sleepers
- diapers and pins or disposable diapers (newborn size)
- plastic pants (unless using disposable diapers)
- sweater, bonnet, and booties (if wearing a gown)
- shawl or blanket, depending on the weather
- infant car seat

A Guide for Birth Companions

Sharing the birth experience is very important and rewarding. You may also want to consider having a second support person. Some knowledge of labour and delivery is useful in helping a woman through labour; however, loving support and companionship are also very important. If you wish to be a birth companion and follow at least some of the suggestions listed below, you will be well on your way to participating in one of the most rewarding experiences of a lifetime.

Before the Birth

- You can start by reading the relevant articles in this handbook! "Rehearsing for Labour" (p. 51), "What to Take to the Hospital" (p. 55), "True Labour and Prelabour — What's the Difference?" (p. 57), "Giving Birth" (p. 60), and "When the Time Comes: Comfort Positions during Labour" (p. 58), all contain useful information for birth companions.
- If possible, arrange to accompany the mother on prenatal visits. During the visits, you can make arrangements to be with her during the birth.
- Accompany the expectant mother to prenatal classes, if at all possible. There, you will learn what to expect during labour and delivery and how to help her with breathing and relaxation techniques. You will also be shown how to help her relieve backache, avoid exhaustion, and take advantage of the time between contractions. In addition, you will learn about positions she can use during labour to help relieve pain.
- It would be a good idea to visit the hospital labour and delivery rooms before the birth to find out about hospital routines and practices. Many hospitals arrange tours and show films or slides to help you get to know their procedures. Sometimes, tours are organized through prenatal classes. While you're at the hospital, you can also find out about the availability of parking, telephone, food, washroom, sleeping area, and anything else you might need. After all, once the big day arrives, you may very well be there for several hours!
- Practise relaxation and breathing techniques with the expectant mother as much as possible.

CALDWELL

During the Birth

- Stay with her. No woman should be left alone during labour. Since the hospital surroundings will be unfamiliar to her, your presence will help make her feel more comfortable.
- Talk to her; tell her she's doing fine and you are confident she will do well. Maintain eye contact and smile at her.
- Encourage her to talk to the baby during the birth. It might be helpful.
  - Breathe with her during her contractions.
    - Sponge her brow, comb her hair, and encourage her to relax between contractions. Try not to get distracted by anything else going on, as this may make her tense.
    - Use the comfort measures (massage, water, cold pack, etc.) suggested in the articles "Rehearsing for Labour" on p. 51 and "Giving Birth" on p. 60.
- To help relieve backache and the pain of contractions, and to speed the progress of labour, encourage her to adopt some of the positions suggested in the article "When the Time Comes: Comfort Positions during Labour" on p. 58.
- Tell her when you first see the baby's head emerging. You may wish to hold up a mirror so she can see the baby emerging.
- If you have moments of being out of control, try to relax and let go. Remember, there is always a nurse or doctor to help you through them.

True Labour and Prelabour — What's the Difference?

CHAPMAN

Madeleine woke up at three a.m. She was having contractions, much more intense than any she'd experienced before. The big moment had finally arrived! She woke up Ben, her husband, and told him to go and start the car. It was time!

In a matter of minutes they were at the hospital, and Madeleine was admitted. Then a strange thing happened. Her contractions started becoming weaker rather than stronger. She asked the doctor who was examining her if that was normal. The doctor looked at her and said she might as well go home. She wouldn't be going into labour for some time yet. Madeleine put on her coat, surprised. It had certainly felt as if she was in labour. What was wrong with her?

There was nothing wrong with Madeleine. She had just made the common mistake of confusing prelabour or "false labour" for true labour. This is a mistake that even women who are doctors or nurses themselves have been known to make. Basically, the contractions associated with prelabour make the uterus contract and relax and are a form of pre-liminary labour. They usually stop after a while, although they can last for hours. If you feel them, get up and walk around and see if they continue or if the intervals between them become longer. If the intervals lengthen, you are probably experiencing prelabour or "false labour." If the intervals between contractions become shorter, on the other hand, you are probably going into true labour.

Confused? The comparison chart below should help.

Prelabour	True labour
Contractions occur at irregular intervals.	Contractions occur at a more regular interval (e.g., 15 to 20 minutes apart, lasting 1/2 minute).
Intervals between contractions remain long.	Intervals between contractions gradually shorten.
Intensity of contractions remains the same.	Intensity of contractions gradually increases.
Contractions are located chiefly in the abdomen.	Contractions can be felt in the abdomen, back, and sometimes in the thighs.
Walking has no effect on contractions, but often gives relief. There is no "show" (blood-tinged mucus). The cervix usually remains closed and unstretched.	Contractions are intensified by walking. Show is usually present. The cervix thins and shortens (effaces) and stretches or opens up (dilates).

When the Time Comes: Comfort Positions during Labour

The following chart shows a variety of positions to help you feel more comfortable during labour. It also describes how to enhance progress during labour. You will want to try these positions ahead of time and keep them in mind, since it is not until you are actually in labour that you will know which will be most helpful.

Position	Benefits
Walking (1st Stage of Labour) 	• combines the effects of gravity and changes in the positioning of the pelvic joints in encouraging the baby's head to move down • helps relieve backache and may make your contractions less painful and more productive
Standing (1st Stage of Labour) 	• encourages the baby to move down and makes your contractions less painful and more productive, but can be tiring if done for long periods • (Leaning forward while standing is more restful and can help relieve backache.) • (Many women find rocking or swaying of the hips to be comforting.)
Sitting Upright (1st & 2nd Stages of Labour) 	• makes use of gravity to help the baby move down, but can aggravate backache and hemorrhoids if used for too long a time • can be a restful change and can be used during electronic fetal monitoring
Semi-Sitting (1st & 2nd Stages of Labour) 	• can slow the arrival of the baby, but you may find it helpful as a resting position • (Sitting on the toilet may help relax the perineum for bearing down.) • (Leaning forward and resting against your partner makes back-rubbing easier.)

Position	Benefits

Kneeling (1st & 2nd Stages of Labour)

- if used for short periods of time, can take the pressure off hemorrhoids and can relieve backache, especially if you try the pelvic tilt in this position (for more information on the pelvic tilt, see description on p. 37)
- (There is less strain on your hands and wrists if you lean forward on a chair or bed.)

Side-lying (1st & 2nd Stages of Labour)

- is a good resting position and, if alternated with walking, can help during the first stage of labour
- takes the pressure off hemorrhoids
- helps you relax between contractions and helps slow down a rapid second stage of labour
- is a safe position if you've taken pain medications
- is recommended by some doctors as a position to adopt for delivery

Squatting

- takes advantage of gravity and widens the pelvic outlet to help the baby descend
- requires less effort than other positions if you do not have a strong urge to push (for more information on this comfort position, see the article "Physical Activity throughout Pregnancy" on p. 23)

It is important to change positions frequently during the first and second stages of labour. World-renowned childbirth educator and social anthropologist, Sheila Kitzinger, states, "Avoid getting stuck in one position; the essence of labour is movement." (S. Kitzinger, *The Complete Book of Pregnancy and Childbirth*, Knopf, 1989.)

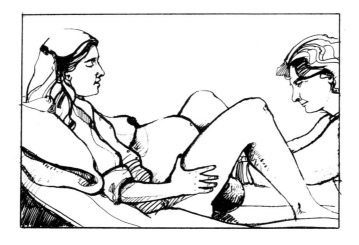

Giving Birth

Just as no two pregnancies are exactly the same, so no two labours will be identical. For instance, it is hard to predict how long you will be in labour. With most first pregnancies, labour lasts for 10 to 14 hours, but for some women, it can last longer; for subsequent births, labour is often less intense and shorter. No matter how long your labour lasts, though, it will occur in four distinct stages. The first of these stages comprises two distinct phases.

You may be surprised to learn that labour does not end with the birth of your baby. Labour continues until the placenta, which has carried nourishment to the baby throughout the pregnancy, is expelled from your body. The following gives more information about what you can expect in labour. It also describes some steps you can take to minimize the discomforts you may experience. For information on how your birth companion can help out during the labour, see the article "A Guide for Birth Companions" on p. 56.

Early First Stage

If you think labour has started — call your doctor.

The early phase is from the start of labour until the cervix opens (or dilates) to approximately 4 cm, about the width of two fingers. During the first stage of labour, the cervix is thinning out (effacing) and opening (dilating).

What will happen to my body?

- Your cervix will thin and shorten, and the opening will stretch from a few millimetres to approximately 4 cm (1 1/2 in.). Your contractions may feel like menstrual cramps and might last about 30 to 45 seconds. It is difficult to define when labour starts (see the article "True Labour and Prelabour — What's the Difference?" on p. 57).
- You may experience backache and pelvic pressure.
- You will probably notice "show" (slightly pinkish mucus discharge).
- You may have some light diarrhea.
- Your membranes could rupture (may occur before labour begins or during 1st or 2nd stages). It can feel like a small trickle or a big gush. If your membranes rupture and you are not in the hospital, call your doctor.

FIRST STAGE OF LABOUR

Cervix prior to effacement or dilation

Beginning of effacement

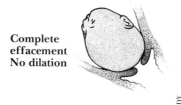

Complete effacement No dilation

CODY

How might I be feeling?

- excited and relieved
- somewhat apprehensive
- sociable and talkative
- between contractions, impatient and eager for progress

What should I do (if in early labour and membranes have not ruptured)?

- Carry on with your usual activities as long as possible (e.g., light housework, writing letters, preparing meals).
- Time the contractions.
- Eat a light meal (if doctor advises).
- Have a warm bath or shower if someone is nearby.
- Alternate activities with rest periods, trying comfort positions and relaxation techniques (see the articles "When the Time Comes: Comfort Positions during Labour" on p. 58 and "Rehearsing for Labour" on p. 51).
- Breathe in a normal manner until you can no longer talk or walk through a contraction. Then begin slow breathing as needed (see "Rehearsing for Labour" on p. 51).

Active First Stage (probably at the hospital)

This stage usually lasts from 4 to 12 hours for the first baby and up to 8 hours for subsequent babies. During this active phase, the cervix opens (dilates) from 4 to 10 cm. The last 5 to 20 contractions are referred to as transition, when the cervix is opening (dilating) the last 2 cm (3/4 in.).

What will happen to my body?

- By now, your contractions may be coming every three to five minutes and lasting 45 to 60 seconds. They will likely become closer, stronger, and of longer duration until they come every two to three minutes and last 60 to 90 seconds each. These long, strong contractions complete dilation.
- Show can increase until it is heavy, dark, and bloody.
- Towards the end of this phase, you may find that:
  — you have momentary nausea and vomiting, natural amnesia, leg cramps, trembling of extremities, backache, and/or perspiration on your forehead and around your eyes
  — you feel hot or cold and restless
  — relaxation is becoming more difficult
  — you feel sleepy and drowsy between contractions
  — you feel rectal pressure and an urge to push. DO NOT PUSH (unless you know the cervix is fully open).

How might I be feeling?

- increasingly serious, quiet, preoccupied with yourself and the labour
- in need of quiet companionship
- having doubts and wondering if you can cope with contractions to come
- as if contractions are hard work, and you would prefer not to talk or be distracted
- then, as the stage progresses, and you move into transition:
  — increasingly irritable, sensitive, and having trouble expressing your needs
  — overwhelmed, and inclined to give up
  — bewildered, frustrated, and temporarily discouraged
  — exhausted
  — as if you cannot bear to be left alone
  — as if concentrating and relaxing during and between contractions is increasingly difficult
  — surprised, overwhelmed, or even frightened at the urge to push
  — suddenly hostile towards those providing support

What should I do?

- Have a warm shower: try sitting on a stool or leaning against your partner or the wall.
- Have a hot water bottle or cold pack (e.g., ice bag) placed on your lower back to ease back pain.
- Use the positions that are most comfortable (see "When the Time Comes: Comfort Positions during Labour" on p. 58).
- Continue using the relaxation techniques that work best for you — focal point concentration/visualization,

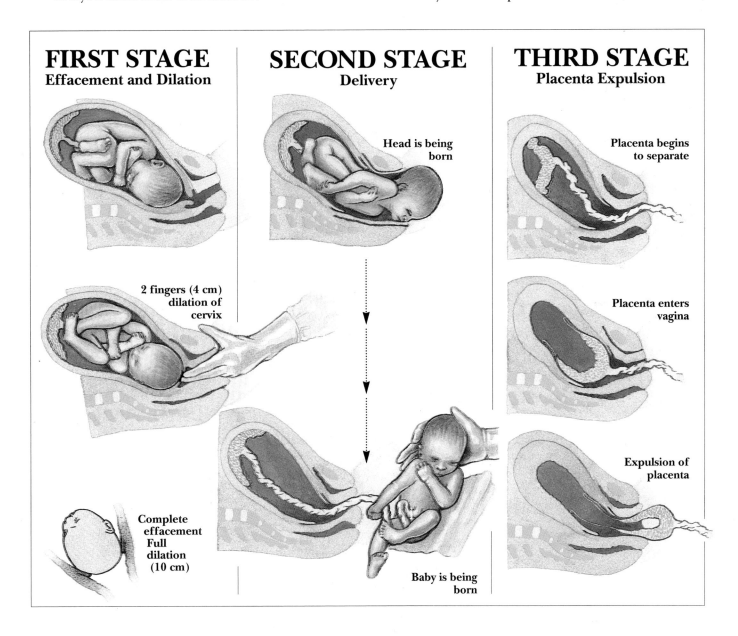

FIRST STAGE
Effacement and Dilation

2 fingers (4 cm) dilation of cervix

Complete effacement Full dilation (10 cm)

SECOND STAGE
Delivery

Head is being born

Baby is being born

THIRD STAGE
Placenta Expulsion

Placenta begins to separate

Placenta enters vagina

Expulsion of placenta

massage, touch relaxation, etc. (see "Rehearsing for Labour" on p. 51).

- Continue slow breathing, using variations as required (see "Rehearsing for Labour").
- Concentrate on one contraction at a time, taking a deep, relaxed breath at the start and end of each contraction.
- Relax and rest between contractions, but remain alert.
- Sip water, tea, or juice between contractions to fulfil your body's requirement for fluids. If the quantities of fluid you can consume are restricted, you could try sucking on ice chips, a wet washcloth, or a sour candy to make your mouth feel less dry. If for medical reasons your doctor does not wish you to have any food or fluids, you may be given fluids through a tube inserted into a vein in your hand or arm (intravenously).
- When contractions become strong and frequent (every two to three minutes), you may feel an irresistible urge to push: DON'T PUSH (unless you know the cervix is fully open). Pant through the peak of the contraction, gradually easing your breathing back to normal as the contraction is over; then take a big breath and let it out slowly, relaxing your whole body as you do so.
- Stay as relaxed as possible.
- Do not tighten your bottom (anus); instead, relax your pelvic floor.

Second Stage/Delivery

The cervix is now fully open. During the second stage of labour, the baby is pushed out through the birth canal. This is the active, hardworking stage of labour. It is not unusual for it to last up to two hours, or more.

The baby usually faces the mother's spine, the head flexing as it moves down. The head then extends to escape under the pubic bone. Your vagina easily stretches to allow the baby to pass through as shown in the illustrations. If necessary, the doctor may do an episiotomy (i.e., make a small cut in the perineum to slightly widen the outer opening of the vagina). This will allow the baby's head to exit more easily. Once the baby is fully out, the doctor places clamps on the umbilical cord and cuts it to separate the baby from the placenta.

What will happen to my body?

- Contractions coming every two to three minutes and lasting 60 to 90 seconds will be powerful and expulsive, but may be further apart. There will be an irresistible urge to push (pushing usually feels good if the perineum is relaxed and you work with the urge to push).
- There may be rectal bulging, and backache may go away.
- As the baby's head moves down the birth canal, there can be groin pressure, a splitting sensation, and a burning feeling. It may feel as if the baby is "stuck."

- As baby's head crowns, you may be asked to stop pushing.
- The baby's head is born. You will be asked to stop pushing while the birth attendant checks to see if the cord is around the baby's neck.
- Wait until you are told to push again.
- The baby's face may appear to be purplish-blue. This is normal.
- The baby's shoulders deliver and the rest of the baby slips out easily.

How might I be feeling?

- surprised, overwhelmed, or frightened by the pushing sensation
- very tired, but experiencing a revival of determination and a burst of energy
- anxious and hesitant to push because of pressure on the rectum
- drowsy and peaceful between contractions
- self-concerned, indifferent to surroundings, excited, absorbed, and/or impatient for progress
- mentally alert and excited (these feelings replacing feelings of drowsiness and discouragement)

What should I do?

- Ease your chin towards your chest and place your tongue on the roof of your mouth (or just relax your tongue).
- Adopt your birthing position (e.g., semi-sitting, squatting, or side-lying).
- Bend your elbows and grip your legs with your hands, or hold hand grips.
- Relax your pelvic muscles.
- Use an appropriate breathing pattern, taking your cue from those helping you. Pant if requested to do so (see "Rehearsing for Labour" on p. 51).
- Rest gently when contractions finish.

Third Stage

During the third stage of labour, the uterus contracts to become smaller, and the placenta completes its separation from the lining of the uterus.

What will happen to my body?

- Contractions temporarily cease after birth, but may resume.
- The uterus rises in the abdomen and takes on a globular shape (grapefruit size).
- The uterus contracts to expel the placenta. This can take between 5 and 20 minutes.
- A gush of blood may precede or accompany the expulsion of the placenta.
- An injection of oxytocin (a hormone that stimulates contraction of the uterus) may be given to help the uterus contract.

- If an episiotomy has been done (see the information given here on the second stage of labour), it will be repaired under local anaesthetic.

What will happen to my baby?
- Your baby will be checked by the doctor and kept warm.
- The doctor will help your baby breathe by removing fluids from the nose and mouth (suctioning) and providing oxygen or extra stimulation, if needed.
- As soon as possible, your baby will be given to you and your partner to cuddle.

How might I be feeling?
- euphoric, ecstatic, relieved, grateful, and/or filled with disbelief, wonder, joy, excitement (some mothers don't experience any particular feeling, though)
- exhausted, but perhaps too excited to notice
- proud and fulfilled
- ravenously hungry and thirsty
- focused on the baby and seeking reassurance that he or she is normal
- sleepy when the excitement subsides (or so excited that you are unable to sleep)
- perhaps unaware of the placenta's expulsion

What should I do?
- Remain relaxed and push gently if needed to expel the placenta.
- Lie back and, together with your partner, enjoy the baby, remembering how important it is to keep baby warm.
- Put the baby to your breast.

The Fourth Stage of Labour

During the first two or three hours after birth, sometimes referred to as the fourth stage of labour, you and the baby will be given extra attention and care as you recover from the hard work of labour and begin this new time in your lives. It is not unusual for mothers to feel chills and tremors, to have difficulty passing urine, and to have discomfort as a result of afterpains, an episiotomy, and/or hemorrhoids. To ease these problems, the nurse can provide a warmed blanket, put an ice pack or warm compresses on the perineum, and offer pain-relief medication.

You will be encouraged to drink reasonable amounts of fluid slowly. After the first hour, you will be encouraged to have a light meal if you feel hungry. You will also be asked to call the nurse before trying to get up for the first time, as it is not unusual to feel dizzy from changes in circulation. During this two- or three-hour period, you may want to continue to cuddle the baby. On the other hand, you may be just as content to let your partner, other family members, or the nursery staff enjoy the baby while you slip into a well-deserved sleep.

Medical Procedures during Childbirth

Intervention may become necessary during your pregnancy or during labour for many reasons. Talk over all possibilities with your doctor so you are prepared. Here is a brief outline of the most common interventions.

Induction

Induction is the stimulation of labour before it begins spontaneously. If you have heart disease, diabetes, hypertension, premature rupture of the membranes, or are clearly overdue, induction may be necessary. The most common type of induction is oxytocin infusion, which stimulates or increases contractions. Oxytocin is normally produced by your body; however, synthetic oxytocin is used. Prostoglandin gel is another product that may be used. Your baby will be monitored electronically (see "Electronic Monitoring" on the next page).

Pain Relief (Analgesia) and Anaesthetics

The pain experienced in childbirth is different for every mother and every labour. Relief can be achieved through the help of a supportive person, appropriate breathing, relaxation, warm bath, showering, changes of position, massage, or visualization (see the article "Rehearsing for Labour" on p. 51). These strategies, however, may not be enough.

There are many types of pain relief available during labour.
- TENS (transcutaneous electronic nerve stimulation): a procedure in which two or four electrodes are placed on the body (e.g., back, abdomen), allowing non-invasive energy to pass through the muscles to help them relax
- Sedatives: given to help the mother relax if she is anxious or tense
- Laughing gas: self-administered gas given by mask to take the edge off the pain

- Narcotics (e.g., Demerol): usually given by injection, for pain relief
- Pudendal block: an injection that numbs the perineum, given at full dilation, often if an episiotomy is necessary
- Local anaesthetic: used for episiotomy repair
- Epidural anaesthesia: a type of pain relief in which a local anaesthetic is administered by means of a small, plastic tube inserted into the space around the spinal cord, providing pain relief from the waist down; may be used for a Caesarean birth, allowing the woman to be fully conscious during the delivery
- General anaesthetic: sometimes necessary for a planned or emergency Caesarean birth; renders you completely unconscious.

Electronic Monitoring

During labour, medical staff may want to listen to your baby's heart rate through electronic fetal monitoring. Electronic monitoring indicates the effects of the contractions on the baby's heart rate.

There are two types of electronic monitoring.

- **External:** Two straps are placed around the mother's abdomen: one picks up the baby's heart rate; the other records the contractions of the uterus. The external monitor measures both the duration and frequency of contractions.
- **Internal:** If closer monitoring of the baby's heart rate is required, an internal electrode may be applied to the baby's head.

Although electronic monitoring may restrict your movement, it does not cause discomfort. To find out more about monitoring, talk with your doctor.

Episiotomy

If necessary, an episiotomy is done near the end of the second stage of labour. An episiotomy is an incision made by the doctor in the perineum to allow more room for the baby to pass through the vaginal opening. The area will feel numb from the pressure of the baby against the perineum, but a local anaesthetic may be given. After delivery of the placenta, the incision is sewn with self-dissolving sutures.

Forceps

If the delivery needs to be hastened (e.g., dramatic rise in blood pressure, signs that the baby is in distress), forceps may be used to deliver the baby. Forceps are spoon-like instruments placed gently on either side of the baby's head. They are used to protect the head or to gently ease the baby out. Forceps can leave red marks or slight bruises on the baby's head, but these soon fade.

Vacuum Extraction

Vacuum extraction is another method used to hasten delivery if the baby is in distress. A vacuum cup is applied to the baby's head. While the mother bears down with contractions, the doctor helps to pull the baby down the birth canal.

Breech Delivery

"Breech" is the name given to the position of the baby when the bottom is down (e.g., buttocks or foot first). The normal position for a baby is head first. Special expertise is required for a breech birth. Many women have safe vaginal breech deliveries; however, Caesarean birth may be recommended if there are complications.

Caesarean Birth

See the article "Birth by Caesarean" on p. 65.

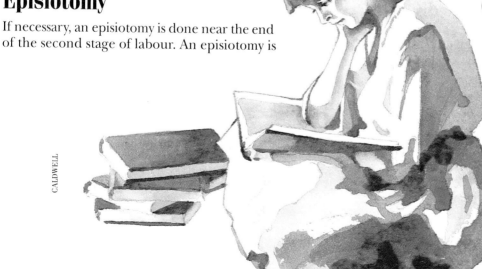

Birth by Caesarean

Babies born by Caesarean birth are delivered through an incision in the abdominal wall and uterus rather than through the vagina. A Caesarean birth is performed in order to protect the life and health of the mother or baby. The circumstances in which a Caesarean birth is likely to be performed include the following.

- The mother's pelvis is too small for the baby to pass through the birth canal.
- The baby is in a breech (bottom or feet first) or transverse (sideways) position, making it difficult to deliver vaginally.
- The dilation of the cervix is prolonged, and the baby's descent through the birth canal is not progressing.
- The baby is in distress. There may be changes in the heart rate, which indicates that the baby isn't getting enough oxygen.
- The baby's cord or placenta is in a position such that the baby's oxygen will be cut off if labour is allowed to continue.
- The placenta has separated from the wall of the uterus, causing bleeding and cutting off oxygen to the fetus.
- The placenta is in an abnormal position.
- The mother has heart problems, high blood pressure, toxemia, diabetes, or has had previous surgery of the uterus.
- The mother has acute herpes lesions or some other vaginal infection that makes vaginal delivery unsafe for the baby.

Options are available to parents expecting a Caesarean birth. For example, if epidural anaesthesia is used, many hospitals allow the birth companion in the delivery room.

If you have had an epidural anaesthetic, you will be able to cuddle your baby and put him or her to the breast almost immediately following delivery. If you have had a general anaesthetic, the birth companion can hold the new baby. Although you may feel a little nauseated from the anaesthetic when you first wake up, you will soon be able to caress and nurse your baby.

Breastfeeding may be more comfortable if you lie on your side or hold the baby using the "football" hold (baby under your arm, by your side, with his or her feet pointing towards your back). If you hold the baby in this manner, you can place a pillow under the baby to provide support and relieve any pressure on the incision.

Following a Caesarean birth, you will be recovering from major surgery as well as the birth of your baby. You may need to ask for help in giving care to the baby, since you will need extra rest to recover from the birth and be successful with breastfeeding. You also need to rest to avoid excessive vaginal discharge of blood, mucus, and tissue from the uterus (called lochia). Some doctors put limitations on activities that may cause tiredness or strain (e.g., climbing stairs, driving, and lifting). Avoid lifting anything that weighs more than your newborn baby. If you have toddlers at home, sit down and have them climb up on your knee.

Generally, you will find that the recovery period is shorter if you are on your feet as soon as possible — ideally, within a day. Pain medication for the first 72 hours may help you move around more readily. Your doctor or a public health nurse in your area can provide an exercise program specially designed for women who have had a Caesarean birth. A good diet and plenty of fluids will help in your recovery as well. It is also important to be kind to yourself. Ask for whatever makes you feel better, whether that's a massage, an ice pack for your incision, or frequent (or fewer) visits from your family and friends. You will definitely need extra help at home during your recovery. Keep in mind that if you try to return to a full program of activities too soon, you will only delay your recovery. Wound healing and strengthening takes about six weeks.

If the Caesarean birth is an emergency situation, you will have no advance warning, yet prenatally you can learn about it from your doctor, prenatal instructor, or public health nurse. Everything happens very quickly. There is often little time to grasp the events and the associated feelings. Parents may feel disappointed, inadequate, or depressed about missing the planned vaginal birth. Mothers have reported a wide range of feelings including guilt, jealousy, depression, and a sense of failure. In the unlikely event that you experience an emergency Caesarean birth, the best way to deal with these feelings is to talk about them as openly and honestly as possible — with your partner, with your doctor, with anyone you trust. Help is available from the public health nurse and from other sources such as Caesarean birth groups.

Perhaps the best tonic for any negative feelings associated with having had an emergency Caesarean birth, is to begin caring for your baby as soon as possible. There is no better way to strengthen your feeling of love for your baby and help you put things in perspective. If you do experience a Caesarean birth, whether it's planned or an emergency, there is one important fact that should be kept in mind. When you deliver your child by Caesarean, you are still giving birth.

Once a Caesarean, Always a Caesarean?

Just because you have had a Caesarean birth in the past does not mean it isn't possible to have a vaginal birth the next time you have a baby. Women can have a trial labour, providing the following conditions are met.
• Your doctor has the records from your previous pregnancy and birth.
• Your pregnancy is normal and uncomplicated.

• The reason for the previous Caesarean birth no longer applies.
• There is only one fetus in the uterus.
• The previous incision was a lower segment transverse cut.

The main concern doctors have is that the uterus will separate at the site of the old incision; however, it is very unlikely that this will happen. In fact, a Vaginal Birth After Caesarean (VBAC) carries a lower risk of infection than a repeat Caesarean birth and can be safer for both mother and baby. This is because there are fewer anaesthesia complications. A vaginal delivery also makes for a shorter hospital stay and a more rapid recovery.

A VBAC is much more likely to be successful if:
• you have had regular prenatal care,
• everyone involved is prepared for the birth, and
• there will be no sense of failure on anyone's part if vaginal birth proves not to be possible.

If you are considering a Vaginal Birth After Caesarean, talk to your doctor. It's important for you to feel that you have made the right choice and that you have confidence in yourself and your doctor. You may also find it helpful to attend VBAC classes.

CHAPMAN

Premature Babies

Premature babies, or "preemies" as they are called in the medical world, are babies born before the thirty-seventh week of pregnancy. Preemies are completely formed, but their organ systems are immature. This means that the body and its complex control systems are not ready to function on their own. Depending on the baby's age, he or she could have any of the following:

- immature lungs, causing breathing difficulties (the baby's breathing may need to be monitored continuously or the baby may need help breathing),
- unco-ordinated sucking and swallowing (feeding may be difficult),
- a liver that is not fully mature (the baby may have jaundice, especially in the first few days of life),
- lower resistance to infection,
- bruising and bleeding because blood vessels are thin and fragile (the baby will need to be handled gently), or
- difficulty maintaining body temperature.

Giving birth to a premature infant may be upsetting and frightening. The preemie may need to be separated from the parents because special care is required. Be assured that your doctor and the hospital staff are supportive and available to talk with you. They can answer your questions and discuss your baby's special needs. Despite the need for added rest, the preemie, like all babies, needs to be touched, stroked, and talked to, even while inside the incubator or isolette.

CHAPMAN

Many hospitals encourage parents to visit and participate in caring for their premature baby. The staff will assist you with learning about feeding and handling your baby and discuss your baby's wake and sleep times with you.

Many parents feel guilty or responsible for the premature birth of their baby, even though no specific cause of prematurity can be found in more than 50 per cent of premature births. In many communities, parent support groups can provide understanding in addition to valuable information and practical assistance for parents coping with a premature infant. Information about support groups and services is available from your local health unit/department.

Low Birth-Weight Babies

In general, birth weight is closely related to the length of the pregnancy; however, approximately one-third of low birth-weight babies (less than 2.5 kg or 5 1/2 lb.) are born at term (40 weeks' gestation).

Some factors that may influence birth weight include:
- sex of the baby,
- height of the mother and father,
- race,
- prenatal care and nutrition,
- maternal smoking, alcohol and drug use, and illness, and
- multiple births.

Low birth-weight babies have special needs and may be cared for in special nurseries. These babies may be kept in incubators to keep them warm and to enable nursing staff to observe them easily. Like premature babies, low birth-weight babies may have problems with breathing. They may also have low blood-sugar levels, at first, and jaundice. Some low birth-weight babies may require special monitoring. Your doctor and the hospital staff will assist you with any questions or concerns. They will also help you to learn about and participate in caring for any special needs your baby may have.

Jaundice

Jaundice appears in about half of full-term infants and about three-quarters of premature infants. It is usually part of the newborn baby's natural adjustment to life after birth. Following birth, the newborn has extra red blood cells that are no longer needed because the baby is now able to breathe air. As the blood cells break down, a yellow-coloured substance (called bilirubin) is formed. Sometimes the baby's liver cannot handle all the bilirubin. The excess in the baby's blood causes the skin and the whites of the eyes to take on a yellowish tinge called jaundice.

In most infants, jaundice is mild and lasts only a few days. However, in more severe cases, the doctor may decide to place your baby under special blue lights (phototherapy) to help reduce the level of bilirubin. When under the lights, the baby's eyes will be protected by a covering. The baby may be sleepier and slower to feed as a result of phototherapy. Also, more frequent feedings may be necessary to replace fluid. The hospital staff are available to discuss these and other special needs your baby has while under phototherapy.

Newborn Screening Program

Certain diseases can be present at birth in apparently healthy newborn babies. If untreated, they can cause irreversible mental retardation, even though baby looks fine in the first few days or even months of life. These diseases include:

- Congenital hypothyroidism: occurs in one out of every 3000 to 4000 babies and is treated by giving the baby a daily pill containing thyroid hormone
- PKU (phenylketonuria hyperphenylalaninemia): occurs in about one in every 18,000 babies and is treated with a special diet
- Galactosemia: occurs in about one in every 30,000 babies and is also treated with a special diet.

All of these diseases can be treated as soon as a diagnosis is made, thus preventing mental retardation. The sooner treatment is started, the better the outcome for the baby.

Before being discharged from the hospital or soon after birth, every baby has a blood test, which is sent for screening. If the screening test is positive, the baby's doctor is notified so that further testing for the baby can be arranged. If subsequent testing indicates the presence of one of these diseases, the baby is given the appropriate treatment.

Information about Circumcision

If your baby is a boy, one of the first decisions you may be faced with is whether to circumcise. Circumcision, or removing the foreskin covering the tip of the male infant's penis, is still customary in some families, countries, and religious groups.

There are many differing opinions on whether circumcision is necessary. There does not appear to be any medical reason for circumcision of a newborn infant, and complications of circumcision do occur occasionally. It is worth noting that the Canadian Pediatric Society *does not recommend* routine circumcision. Further, the cost of routine circumcision is generally not covered by provincial medical plans.

In the uncircumcised baby, regular bathing will keep the penis adequately clean. The foreskin should *not* be pushed back to expose the penis. By age three to five years, the foreskin usually separates naturally, so it can easily be pulled back for bathing purposes. However, the foreskin should always be replaced after bathing to keep the penis covered.

If you do decide to have your baby circumcised, here are some steps to take to promote healing and comfort.
- Some doctors will use a petroleum jelly dressing, which should be left on. It helps to control bleeding and keeps the diaper from sticking to the circumcision site. The dressing will fall off within one to two days. It will need to be changed if soiled with a bowel movement.
- Change the baby's diaper frequently.
- Sterile petroleum jelly (e.g., Vaseline) can be placed on the penis to prevent it from sticking to the diaper.
- After the dressing falls off, look closely at the penis for signs of bleeding or infection. You will normally see a whitish yellow substance around the head of the penis for two or three days. Do not remove this. It is a sign that healing is occurring.
- The penis can be gently washed and patted dry at diaper changes after the dressing is off.
- Check to be sure your son is urinating about six to eight times a day.
- Lay the baby on his side.

Learning How to Breastfeed

Breastfeeding is the natural and healthy way to feed your baby. Breastfeeding is a skill that you and your baby will learn with practice. Your baby's first few weeks of life are an important time for developing and practicing these skills.

In societies where most women breastfeed, families and friends give reassurance, support, and information. Ask a family member who has successfully breastfed and/or a lactation consultant or other knowledgeable health professional to help you learn how in the hospital.

Once you're home, call on friends or relatives who have successfully breastfed to talk things over and give you help and support when you need it. Other community people who can give you information, help, and assurance once you're at home with your baby are public health nurses, breastfeeding support groups or La Leche League mothers, lactation consultants or breastfeeding clinics. Use their help and support — women all over the world have always used help and support when they were learning how to breastfeed successfully.

When you breastfeed you develop a satisfying relationship with your baby.

Here are some important things to know and do:
- Tell care staff at the hospital you are breastfeeding and not to give your baby anything to drink — your baby doesn't need anything but your milk (not even pacifiers).
- Put your baby to the breast as soon as possible after birth; babies are more alert and will seek out the breast in their first two hours. Your baby's suckling starts your milk production. Skin-to-skin contact is important, so have your baby unwrapped during feeding. Some mothers use a kangaroo pack to keep their babies next to their bodies all of the time.

Important Words

- **Areola:** the dark part of the breast
- **Colostrum:** the first "milk" you produce after your baby is born
- **Latching:** bringing the baby and the breast together so he or she can get the milk out of the breast and into his or her mouth
- **"Let down":** the prickly, rushing feeling that tells you that the milk in your breast is there for the baby to drink
- **Positioning:** how you hold the baby so you can be comfortable and the baby can get your breast in his or her mouth properly (latch)
- **Suckling:** what babies do at the breast to get milk

Colostrum

Colostrum, your first "milk," is very rich and gives your baby nutrition and protection against sickness. Most women have a small amount of this important first milk. This is usual and it is all your newborn baby needs. Women who have Caesarean births should breastfeed their babies as soon as possible after birth. Some mothers don't feel "let down."

The First Feedings

Wash your hands, if you can, and get into a comfortable position. Ask your nurse or lactation consultant to help you and your baby to breastfeed. You can lie down or sit. If your bottom is sore, ask for an ice bag to ease the pain. Unwrap your baby so baby's skin can touch yours.

Ask for help to get your baby to latch. To feed your baby, hold your baby at breast height (see the illustrations of different positions). You may need a pillow across your lap to rest your baby on. Use a foot stool if you are sitting in

Modified Cradle Hold

Cradle Hold

Football Hold

Side Lying

GRACE HOSPITAL

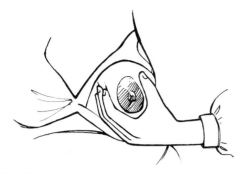

Hand Position for Modified Cradle Hold and Cradle Hold

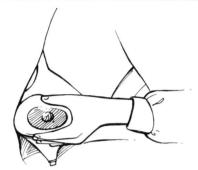

Hand Position for Side Lying and Football Hold

a chair. Have your baby's tummy facing yours and tuck your baby in close. Cup your breast in your free hand with your fingers underneath and your thumb on top (making a C-shape). Be sure your fingers are behind the areola (the dark part of your breast). Touch your baby's lower lip with your nipple until your baby's mouth opens wide like a big yawn. Centre your nipple on the baby's mouth and bring your baby on to your breast so that baby's mouth covers most of the areola — this is latching. Continue to hold your breast during the feeding. Remember that breastfeeding shouldn't hurt. If it does after the first few suckles, break the suction with your finger and try latching again.

Most babies suckle in a pattern and have rest periods in between. Watch for the suck, swallow, breathe pattern. A little rest with closed eyes doesn't mean your baby is asleep. When babies are suckling and swallowing milk, their ears

Latching

move a little. Let your baby decide when to stop feeding. Your baby will let go of the nipple.

Keep your baby with you (rooming in) so that you can breastfeed as often as baby wants. This could be eight to ten times a day. This is important in order to start a good milk supply.

Expect to wake in the night to feed your baby — even while you are in the hospital. Sleep when your baby sleeps.

As Both of You Become More Familiar with Breastfeeding

Remember normal hygiene. Bathe daily (soaps and lotions on your nipples can overdry them). Wash your hands after using the bathroom or changing your baby's diaper.

Feed your baby on a soft breast. If your breast is full and hard, use a warm wet washcloth on your breast or take a shower; massage your breast; and/or express some milk to soften the areola. This will make it easier for your baby to latch and feed well.

For the first few weeks, support your breast while your baby feeds. Soon your baby will be able to suckle strongly and well enough to stay on the breast without your help.

"Let down" may take a few minutes at first, but after the first few feedings it is usually felt in 30 seconds. Anxiety can delay "let down" of milk to the nipple. (See question about "let down" on p. 84.)

Let your baby finish at the first breast before you switch to the other side. It's time to change when your breast feels softer *and* your baby isn't content anymore. Babies may become wiggly at the breast if they need burping.

Babies fall away from the breast when they have had enough. Don't rush — your baby may be resting and not yet finished.

Breastfeeding provides complete nutrition for your baby when you feed on demand (feeding when your baby is hungry). Some babies feed very often at first and then go for a longer time between feeds.

Some very sleepy babies are not very interested in feeding. Do not let your young baby sleep longer than four to five hours without feeding. Discuss this situation with your public health nurse or doctor.

You and your baby are on your way now. Breastfeeding will be easy and convenient after the two of you have practiced it for these first few weeks. Ask for help when you need it. Learn what works for you. You will have no bottles or formula to buy or carry around, just nature's perfect food delivered fresh and safe when your baby needs it.

Some good books are: *Bestfeeding: Getting Breastfeeding Right for You* by Mary Renfrew, Chloe Fisher, and Suzanne Arms, and *The Womanly Art of Breastfeeding* by La Leche League International.

What Should I Eat When I'm Breastfeeding?

Choose healthy foods from the "Food Guide for Pregnancy and Breastfeeding" on p. 16. Enjoy regular meals and snacks and about 2 litres (8 cups) of fluid including water, juice, milk, and soup each day. Here, a registered dietitian-nutritionist answers commonly asked food-related questions:

Can I drink coffee now?

Nutritionist: It is still wise to limit caffeine to two mugs of coffee or four cups of tea daily. Limit cola soft drinks, chocolate, cocoa, cold remedies, and headache relievers that contain caffeine.

Can I drink alcohol now?

Nutritionist: It is best to avoid wine, beer, and spirits as long as you breastfeed your baby. No safe amount is known.

Are there foods I should avoid?

Nutritionist: Eat foods you enjoy. If you suspect a food may be upsetting your baby, talk to a public health nurse or a registered dietitian-nutritionist.

How can I lose the extra weight I put on?

Nutritionist: You will get back to your pre-pregnancy weight, but it takes time. Losing weight quickly is not a good idea while breastfeeding. Some of your weight gain during pregnancy was stored as fat. These fat stores will be used to produce your milk, leading to gradual weight loss. Follow the "Food Guide for Pregnancy and Breastfeeding" on p. 16. Choose physical activities you enjoy. Walking, bike riding, dancing, and swimming are great ways to firm up (see "Physical Activity throughout Pregnancy" on p. 21).

Do I need to continue to take iron or other supplements?

Nutritionist: Not usually, but the need for vitamins and minerals is individual. Discuss this with your doctor, public health nurse, or a registered dietitian-nutritionist.

How can I save time and energy when making meals?

Nutritionist:
- Make one-dish meals using canned or convenience foods.
- Prepare dinner in the morning (e.g., oven or slow-cooker meals).
- Make twice as much as you need and freeze the extra.
- Accept offers of help from neighbours or your family. Ask them to make and serve you a meal.
- Have ready-to-eat foods available in your fridge (for example, cut-up vegetables, a toss-together salad, cheese chunks, hard-cooked eggs, fresh fruit, blender drinks, dried fruit, or muffins).

Remember: Your breastmilk is the very best food for your baby. Eat well, be active, and feel good about yourself. Relax and know your baby is getting the best.

CARNES

Bathing Your Baby

It isn't necessary to give your baby a full bath every day; however, the baby's face, mouth, neck, and bottom should always be washed daily, and you should make sure all skin folds are clean and dry.

For the first bath, it helps if you have support (i.e., your partner or other persons to help you). A baby bath is often demonstrated in the hospital (if you have concerns, a public health nurse can assist). The room should be warm, 22 to 27°C (72 to 80°F), and free from drafts. After taking off any jewellery that might scratch the baby, you should wash your hands and then assemble the equipment. Suggested items include:

- mild soap
- cotton balls
- a washcloth
- a second washcloth or gauze for cleaning the baby's mouth
- alcohol for cleaning around the cord
- cotton-tipped applicators
- diaper pins with safety metal ends (unless using disposable diapers)
- two large soft towels.

If you're bathing the baby on a table, the surface should be at a comfortable working height and protected with heavy plastic, if it is not already waterproof. A blanket, pad, or towel next to the bath will provide a comfortable area for the baby. The water for the bath should be about 37°C (98°F). You can test it with your inner arm to make sure it's comfortably warm. Never leave your baby alone on the table or in the bath. When reaching for anything, always keep one hand on baby.

The best way to bathe your baby is to start at the top and work down! So begin with your baby's face, gently wiping it clean with a fresh, warm washcloth, without soap. There is no need to do anything to the eyes, ears, and nose unless there is some discharge. If there is discharge in your baby's eyes, use the corner of a clean washcloth or a fresh cotton ball to wipe each eye from the inner corner out. Use a separate cotton ball or part of the cloth for each eye. To clean the ears, gently rotate the twisted end of a moist cloth or piece of cotton in the *outer* part of the ear only. If the baby has a runny nose, you can wipe it, leaving the removal of any crusting until the end of the bath, as this usually makes the baby cry. Any crusting can be gently removed with a damp piece of cotton. The use of rigid cotton-tipped applicators is not recommended for cleaning your baby's eyes, ears, or nose. Such applicators can easily damage the delicate linings of these areas.

The next area requiring attention is your baby's scalp. You can either work up a lather of soap on your hands and apply it, or use a mild baby shampoo. Then pick up your baby with one arm, supporting the head with your hand. Rinse off the baby's head over the tub, and dry it gently and thoroughly. If the baby's scalp is dry, you may wish to apply some non-perfumed oil to the scalp and gently massage it in. The natural state for a baby's scalp is mildly scaly; however, if the scalp is crusty, apply a non-perfumed oil, then wash the scalp using a soft washcloth. If oil is left on the scalp, it may cause a build-up of oil and dried skin known as cradle cap. Check with your doctor or a public health nurse if you have any concerns.

Now place your baby in the tub to wash the body, arms, and legs. Talk reassuringly to your baby as you do this. Remember to maintain a firm hold, supporting the head at all times.

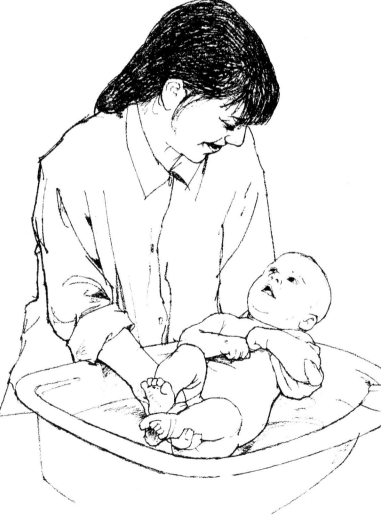

Apply soap, front and back, from the shoulders to the toes and rinse off well with the washcloth. The genital area is washed last. There is no need to push back and cleanse under the foreskin of uncircumcised baby boys. If your baby has been circumcised, follow the instructions given by the hospital staff.

Maintaining the same hold, transfer your baby out of the tub to a waiting towel on the pad. Wrap the towel around your baby and pat dry gently. Make sure you dry all folds and creases of the skin. It is not necessary to use powder as it can irritate the skin, cause bacterial growth, or be inhaled by your baby. As soon as the baby's upper body is dry, you can put on the baby's undershirt or T-shirt. The groin and genital area needs to be cleaned and dried carefully to prevent irritation. To do this, use a piece of cotton or the corner of a towel. Wipe towards the anus, using a fresh piece of cotton for each stroke. Cord care is the next step. Clean the cord starting at the base with cotton-tipped applicators saturated with rubbing alcohol.

Dress your baby, beginning with the diaper. Remember, the diaper should be placed below the navel to prevent cord irritation when the diaper gets wet. Cosy sleepers or a gown will keep baby snug. You can finish by wrapping a warm blanket around the baby. Warm and snug, your baby will enjoy having his or her hair brushed; however, nails are better cut with blunt-ended scissors when your baby is asleep or at least sleepy.

As an alternative to the bath just described, you can give your baby an all-over sponge bath on the pad.

On the other hand, it may be impossible or impractical to bathe your baby using either of these methods. In this case, you could try the "three-in-one" approach: one parent sits in the family bath tub while the other passes the baby in for bathing. With this approach, the baby may cry less and feel more secure. When the bath is finished, the parent inside the bath can pass the baby out to the other parent. He or she can conclude the bathing process as previously described.

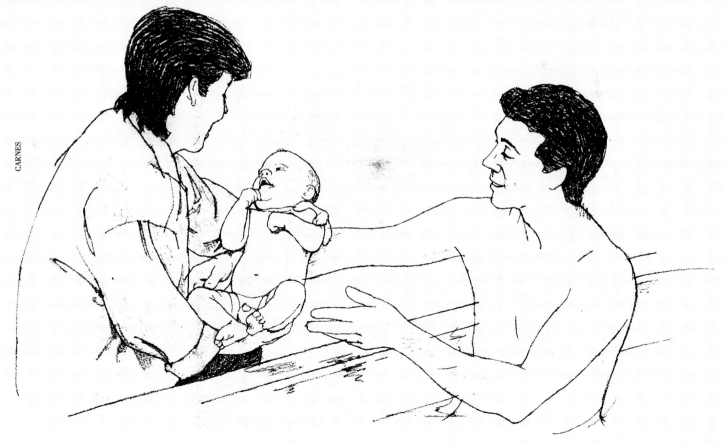

CARNES

Dealing with Diaper Rash

Diaper rash refers to a number of conditions that vary in severity and cause a baby's diaper area to be raw and red-looking. Most often, diaper rash is caused by the ammonia in the urine or by the burning effect of a loose, acidic bowel movement. However, some diaper rashes can result from an allergic reaction to materials, soaps, powders, perfumes, or oils in contact with the skin. Still others are due to a yeast infection, which may spread from the mouth or intestinal tract. Yeast infections can develop after a diaper rash has been present for several days.

It is rare to find a child who has not experienced some diaper rash, but the best cure is still prevention. One factor that affects diaper rash is heat, which encourages bacteria to flourish. Airtight, waterproof pants are, therefore, not a good idea. They trap the urine or stools and increase heat in the diaper area. Use a diaper cover that allows air to enter (e.g., cotton, wool, or polyester).

Check for wetness and soiling often and change the baby when needed. Wash the baby's diaper area with plain or soapy water. Rinse it well and dry gently at *every* changing. Purchased diaper wipes, although convenient, are expensive. As well, they may cause or further irritate diaper rash. Some babies are sensitive to perfume or baby-care products; therefore, it is useful to experiment with different products or eliminate as many as possible if a rash develops.

One of the best remedies for diaper rash is exposure to the air three or four times a day. Air helps dry the skin and heal the rash. A diaper cream applied following airing will promote healing as well. If diaper rash persists in spite of your best efforts to eliminate it, contact your doctor or public health nurse for further advice.

Diapering Tips

Diapering time can be a special time for talking, laughing, and playing with your baby. Prepare ahead for diaper changing and allow time to make it fun. Following are some useful tips for diapering.
- Never leave the baby unattended during changing time. Babies tend to move around, so keep creams, pins, etc., out of reach. Giving your child a soft toy or something to watch will keep an active baby entertained.
- Change baby's diaper whenever it's wet or soiled.
- Wash the diaper area with warm water at every change for a newborn and a few times a day for an older baby.
- Pat dry or allow to air dry.

- Apply a diaper cream as required.
- Wash your hands after each change.
- Safety pins pushed into a bar of soap are easier to pin into the diaper.
- Powder should be used with caution. A puff of powder into the face or nostrils can result in choking and breathing difficulty.

Laundering Tips

Diapers may be soaked in a diaper pail until there are enough to be laundered. They can then be put in the washing machine. Here are some helpful tips for laundering.
- Fill the diaper pail three-quarters full of water and add 175 mL (3/4 cup) vinegar (not chlorine bleach).
- Rinse soiled diapers in the toilet; wet diapers need not be rinsed.
- Rinse the diaper pail before refilling; disinfect occasionally with a solution of 175 mL (3/4 cup) vinegar and 2 L (1/2 gal.) hot water.
- Diaper-pail deodorizing tablets are often a curiosity for your children. If you use these tablets, keep the pail out of reach of your children. In case of accidental ingestion, call your poison control centre.
- When the diaper pail is full, empty the contents into washing machine and spin out excess water.
- Fill the machine to the highest water level, using hot water.
- Use a phosphate-free detergent or a biodegradable soap (pure soap will not wash out well in hard water).
- Run diapers through an extra rinse at the end of the cycle during the first few months, or if your baby is prone to rash.
- Dry diapers in the dryer on a hot setting to prevent bacteria, or hang to dry. (Many diapers will stay softer if put in a dryer for 15 minutes, then hung outside on a line or rail to finish drying.)
- Sunshine is a natural disinfectant and will help cleanse cloth diapers.

Protecting Your Baby from Harm

In getting your home ready for your baby, you should recognize that babies learn by touching, feeling, turning, reaching, and experimenting. Your baby will begin learning this way almost immediately. Your baby is completely dependent on others and unable to recognize dangers, so you will have to protect him or her from harmful situations and objects. What may be safe for the newborn baby may not be safe for very long. The following safety precautions should be taken *immediately*.

- Make sure carpeting on stairs is securely fastened and avoid loose rugs in high-traffic areas. You might slip while carrying the baby.
- Be sure toys are sturdy, non-toxic, washable, and made of materials that do not burn easily. Toys that are large, soft, and have no removable small parts are best. Toys sold in Canada must comply with regulations administered by the Product Safety Branch of Consumer and Corporate Affairs Canada.
- Keep pins (e.g., large diaper pins), needles, buttons, coins, marbles, and disc batteries out of reach and in safe containers.
- Be sure soothers or pacifiers are made in one piece so they can't break apart into smaller fragments. Also, make sure that they are large enough not to be swallowed. Examine them daily and throw them away if they are cracked, show signs of wear, or if the texture or colour changes. Cords and ties *must not* be attached to soothers and placed around a baby or child's neck.
- Keep all small objects out of the crib and out of reach.
- Never leave your baby alone on a table, couch, or bed. Even an adult bed with guard rails is dangerous since an infant can slip through the rails or become caught. To be absolutely safe, put your baby down on the floor.

ORESNIK

- Never leave your baby alone with a toddler, with a jealous pet, with a bottle propped in the mouth (due to the danger of choking), or on a water bed (due to the danger of suffocation).
- Never hold the baby while smoking, drinking a hot drink, or handling a hot utensil.
- Never shake or throw your baby in anger. Such handling can seriously injure the infant's fragile neck or damage the brain. If you feel angry with your baby, talk to someone who can help you to deal with these emotions (e.g., your doctor, support persons, a public health nurse).
- Keep your baby in a safe crib with the sides up, or in a playpen, when not being handled. The crib should have maximum spaces of 6 cm (2 3/8 in.) between the rungs, to prevent an infant from slipping through feet first and getting caught by the head (see the article "Getting Baby Equipment" on p. 78). The crib should also be kept away from long mobiles, blinds, or curtain cords.
- Make sure all baby equipment meets safety standards (see "Getting Baby Equipment" on p. 78).
- Be aware of the first aid procedure for dealing with choking. Baby Saver courses are offered through many community recreation centres. St. John Ambulance and Red Cross ChildSafe Programs that teach basic first aid and provide home safety information are also available in many communities. For more information, see the article "A Guide to Further Resources" at the back of this handbook.
- Keep your poison information centre or hospital number posted along with other emergency numbers so that you have quick access to them in an emergency.
- The Sudden Infant Death Syndrome, also known as SIDS or crib death, is the sudden and unexpected death of a previously healthy infant less than one year of age. Medical authorities have recognized new evidence showing that the "tummy-down" sleeping position is associated with an increased risk of SIDS. While it is likely that there are a variety of causes of SIDS, it is recommended that healthy, full-term infants be positioned on their backs or sides for sleep.

Baby on Board: Car Seat Safety

In Canada, auto accidents kill more than 70 children under the age of five every year. As a parent, you can take steps to avoid having your child become a tragic statistic.

Buying and correctly using an approved car seat is the first step — an important one. It is estimated that the use of correctly installed approved infant car seats could prevent 63 of the 70 deaths noted above. Buckling your baby into the car seat for every ride, even on the very first ride home from the hospital, is important. It is also important to make sure you use the seat correctly.

In Canada, infant car seats are required by law and must meet Canadian Motor Vehicle Safety Standards (CMVSS). Following are some useful and practical hints for buying a car seat.

- Look for the CMVSS label. Do not buy a car seat in the United States — it will not have the CMVSS label.
- Look for a car seat that is easy to use *and* fits in your car.
- Make sure the car seat can be securely fastened in your type of car.
- Be sure your car's lap belt is long enough to go through the frame or over the car seat according to the instructions (all child safety seats are fastened by the car's seat belt).
- If your car has a continuous lap-shoulder belt system, you will need a "locking clip" to hold the car seat in position.
- Look for harness straps that have lots of room for growth and are easily adjusted.

CHAPMAN

- If you're buying a convertible seat, look for a good-sized seat — imagine it fitting a three- or four-year-old.
- Look for a seat you like and will use correctly every time you go out in the car.

If purchasing a used car seat, make sure it is an approved seat and that the manufacturer's instructions are available. Make sure also that the plastic shell is not cracked, the harness is not frayed or torn, and the seat has not been in an accident. The car seat should be new enough that all the locking apparatus continues to be safe.

There are three types of car child safety seats — infant, convertible, and booster seats.

The infant seat is for infants from birth to 9 kg (20 lb.) or about nine months. This seat must be used in the rear-facing position. If a crash occurs, the rear-facing position will distribute the crash force across the baby's back and prevent the baby's neck from flexing forward.

The convertible seat is to be used rear-facing for an infant up to 9 kg (20 lb.) or about nine months, and until the baby can also sit well alone (around nine months). Then it is to be turned around to a front-facing position. This type of seat can be used until your child weighs 18 kg (40 lb.) and is about 100 cm (40 in.) tall. When used in the forward-facing position, it must be tethered. All convertible seats sold in Canada are equipped with a tether strap assembly that bolts the top of the seat to the vehicle frame; the car lap belt is used to secure the bottom of the seat. These two straps help limit the forward or sideways movement of the seat in an accident.

The booster seat is used for children from 18 to 27 kg (40 to 60 lb.) who have outgrown their convertible seat.

If you want to rent a car seat rather than buy one, contact your local health unit/department for the names of rental or loaner programs in your community. For more information, see the article "A Guide to Further Resources" at the back of this handbook.

Once you have chosen your car safety seat, it is important to install and use it correctly. Here are important points to remember:
- Place the infant seat in the car so that the baby faces the rear of the vehicle.
- Install the infant seat in the front passenger seat if you wish to watch your baby. Otherwise, install it in the centre of the back seat. If you have a car with a passenger-side airbag, keep the child restraint in the back seat, stopping to check your baby if another adult is not present.
- If the vehicle seat slopes, level the infant seat with a rolled towel when carrying a newborn or very small baby. This prevents the infant from slumping forward in the harness. Remove the towel when the infant can hold its head upright.
- If using a convertible seat, follow the manufacturer's recommendations when using the rear-facing or front-facing position.

- Secure the infant seat or convertible seat to the car snugly using the vehicle lap belt or lap-shoulder belt as shown in the manufacturer's instructions.
- Attach a locking clip to hold the infant seat or convertible seat firmly in position if your vehicle has a continuous lap-shoulder belt with a free-sliding latch plate. Check the manufacturer's instructions for the correct use of the locking clip.

Correctly harnessing your baby in the rear-facing infant seat or convertible seat is also important. Remember:
- Before using a car seat, dress the baby in clothes with arms and legs (i.e., no buntings).
- Place the baby's bottom against the back of the seat. Add rolled towels outside the harness to support the infant's head and body or use a purchased "head hugger." For very small babies, use a seat without a lap pad or shield because these may come into contact with the baby's face and neck.
- Fasten the harness snugly around the infant. If more than two fingers fit between the shoulder straps and the baby's collarbone, the harness needs to be tightened.
- Position the chest clip (if there is one) at the level of the underarms. The chest clip holds the harness straps in place on the shoulders.
- For convertible seats with a five-point harness system, keep the crotch strap short so the hip straps will be over the pelvis and not up on the stomach.
- Raise the harness straps to the upper slots in the seat back when the infant's shoulders are level with or above the lower slots.
- Double back all harness straps that pass through buckles to prevent them from slipping under tension.
- For extra warmth, place a blanket over the harness, not underneath.
- Buckle your child into the car seat before *every* trip, no matter how short.

Read the manufacturer's instructions for correct installation and use of your car seat. Check your vehicle owner's manual — especially for information on how to tether the forward-facing car seat. For additional information, consult your car dealership or your local health unit/department. As well, see the article "A Guide to Further Resources" at the back of this handbook.

When you leave the car for any reason, take time to unbuckle the safety restraint and bring your child with you. An infant or toddler should *never* be left alone in a vehicle!

When travelling on an airplane with an infant or young child, it is recommended that parents use a car seat. Most car seats today can be used on airplanes (check the manufacturer's instructions). Airlines are not required to let parents use them, so it is best to ask for approval and get written confirmation from the airline when making your reservations. You may be able to use your car seat if you travel on a low-volume flight, but some airlines may require you to buy an additional ticket.

Getting Baby Equipment

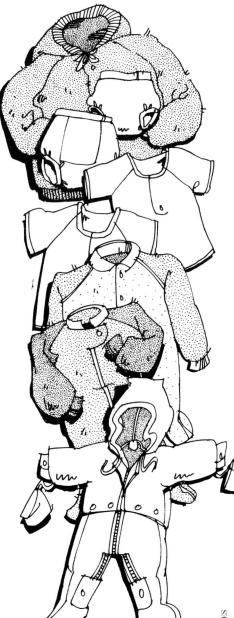

CARNES

What equipment do you need to get ready for the baby? Whatever you choose will probably depend on such things as finances, availability of space, family and community customs, and your own preferences. Some items can be homemade or obtained through friends, relatives, next-to-new shops, and garage sales. The most important considerations are safety and comfort.

Be cautious and careful when purchasing or receiving second-hand gifts such as cribs, strollers, and car seats as they may not meet current government safety standard specifications. Also, items only a few years old can be in poor condition or have a hazardous design feature. Under the *Hazardous Products Act,* it is illegal to sell cribs, playpens, and strollers if they do not meet the requirements of the applicable regulations. When buying or receiving second-hand equipment, make sure the instructions are included. If you have any doubts, consider a new purchase.

If you need more information than is supplied here, contact your health unit or the local office of Consumer and Corporate Affairs Canada (e.g., for safer sleepwear regulations, especially if you are sewing). The following list will give some idea of what your baby might need. You may be wise to get only the essentials before the birth.

Clothing

The clothing you buy for your baby will depend on the time of year and on your laundry facilities. Since babies grow quickly, it is best to purchase clothes in infant sizes of six months to one year. Remember that any clothing that has been stored with mothballs must be washed until no smell remains when wet.

Here is a list of possible purchases:
- undershirts: four (shirts with front ties, grippers, or extra shoulder-opening space are easiest to put on; avoid buttons or tight neckbands),
- nightgowns, sleepers, or stretch suits: three or four,
- waterproof pants: three or four (diaper covers are also available in polyester, wool, or cotton should your child develop rashes with plastic),
- sweaters: one, and
- snowsuit with legs: one (depending on the season).

Diapers

The variety of diaper styles and materials available has expanded immensely. Some families are finding cloth as con-venient as disposable varieties. Below are some considerations to assist you in making your decision.
- A baby will be in diapers for about two and a half years.
- A baby is diapered approximately 6000 times before being trained (in two and a half years).
- Cloth diapers laundered at home are the cheapest.
- Diaper services are generally more expensive than home laundry, but cheaper than disposables overall.
- If buying cloth diapers, three to four dozen will be required, since they are reusable.
- If buying disposable diapers, approximately 6000 will be required.
- If purchasing disposable diapers, buy only one package to start in case your baby in unable to wear them.

- Some fitted cloth diapers accommodate more growth than others. (Be aware that some diapers don't grow with your baby and are, therefore, very expensive.)
- Square or rectangular cloth diapers can be folded to fit a baby as it grows.
- When purchasing diapers, consider absorbency (the ability to draw moisture away from skin), fit (to prevent rubbing and leakage), and convenience (Velcro, snaps, clips, diaper pins, etc.).
- With cloth diapers, you will need a diaper pail.
- The volume of garbage created with disposable diapers is an environmental concern in some communities.

For more information on diapering and laundry tips, see the article "Dealing with Diaper Rash" on p. 74.

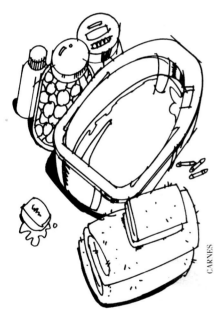

CARNES

Bath Equipment

You will need a basin or sink in which to bathe your baby, as well as two large, soft towels and two washcloths. It is also a good idea to prepare a box or tray for the baby's bath supplies. It may contain:
- mild soap in a dish (a soap bar cut into smaller pieces lasts longer),
- cotton balls in a jar (avoid using cotton-tipped applicators, since a sharp poke can hurt the baby's delicate skin),
- alcohol for cleaning around the cord (keep away from toddlers),

- diaper pins with safety metal ends (so they don't open unexpectedly), unless you're using diapers that come with other fasteners, and
- skin-protecting cream for the baby's bottom (optional).

Furniture and Bedding

You will not require much furniture for a new baby's room. However, you may find a rocking chair useful in providing some pleasant time for you and your baby. You will need a small chest of drawers or a box to store clothing in, and a crib, cradle, bassinet, basket, or sturdy box for your baby to sleep in. Most parents find that a crib is essential once their child becomes active, so you might want to consider getting one right at the start.

You need to carefully choose a suitable crib or cradle for your baby. The federal government no longer supplies information on how to update an older

crib. Parents should not use a crib that doesn't meet the federal government's *Cribs and Cradles Regulations (1986)*. Make sure that each part of the crib is properly and securely in place at all times. Follow manufacturer's instructions when assembling. Cribs should also have double locks for securing the "drop" side (see the diagram below). Check for manufacture date — most cribs made before 1986 do not meet regulations and are not safe!

Mattresses

Some mattresses are too small for their cribs and don't fit the frame properly. This can leave a gap along the side or end of the crib. If the baby gets his or her head stuck between the mattress and the end of the crib, suffocation could result. The gap between the mattress and the sides or ends of the crib shouldn't be any wider than 3 cm (1 1/8 in.) when the mattress is pushed into one corner of the crib. The mattress

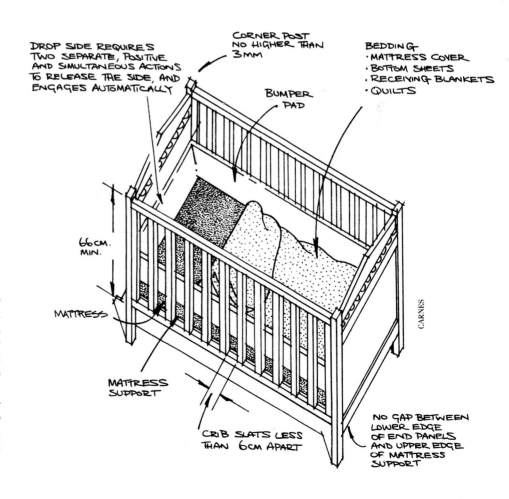

DROP SIDE REQUIRES TWO SEPARATE, POSITIVE AND SIMULTANEOUS ACTIONS TO RELEASE THE SIDE, AND ENGAGES AUTOMATICALLY

CORNER POST NO HIGHER THAN 3MM

BEDDING
- MATTRESS COVER
- BOTTOM SHEETS
- RECEIVING BLANKETS
- QUILTS

BUMPER PAD

66CM. MIN.

MATTRESS

MATTRESS SUPPORT

CRIB SLATS LESS THAN 6CM APART

NO GAP BETWEEN LOWER EDGE OF END PANELS AND UPPER EDGE OF MATTRESS SUPPORT

CARNES

should not be any thicker than 15 cm (6 in.). If they are soft or worn or have a tear, they are dangerous. Very young babies are able to move and may be easily trapped, or choke.

The mattress support system should hold firmly and be checked regularly. You can do this by shaking the mattress support, thumping the mattress from the top, and pushing hard on the support from underneath. This is very important! Make sure all screws, locks, and clamps are tight.

Crib Bumper Pads

Bumper pads are used to protect the baby's head if it bumps against the side of the crib. A bumper pad that protects on all four sides of the crib is the safest, but only if it is securely attached at various points. Securing ties should not be any longer than 15 cm (6 in.).

Many bumper pads come protected with a plastic cover. This cover should be checked as often as possible. If the cover is punctured or torn, it could be chewed or torn even further. A baby might swallow or inhale pieces of the plastic and choke. A torn cover can also lead to holes in the bumper pad. Babies have been known to stick their heads in those holes and suffocate. As soon as your baby can stand, remove the bumper pads and any large toys that could be used as steps for climbing (and falling).

Bedding

The most important considerations when choosing bedding for an infant or toddler are safety, warmth, and ease. To protect the crib mattress, you can use either a quilted crib pad (one side waterproof) or a mattress cover, placed under the sheets. Plastic sheets should not be used since they could hamper breathing. A supply of bottom sheets (fitted — optional) will also be needed for the crib. Pillow cases can be used for a bassinet or carriage. Four or so receiving blankets, along with two or three baby blankets (see "Keeping Your Baby at a Comfortable Temperature on p. 108) should complete your bedding. True top sheets, in which the infant could become entangled, are generally

only recommended for older toddlers.

Any mobiles or other toys strung across cribs and playpens should be well out of your baby's reach. These items should be removed as soon as the baby can sit up or push up on hands and knees. This prevents the danger of baby chewing on unsafe objects or becoming tangled in the mobile or other toys.

When your baby is taller than 90 cm (36 in.) or able to climb out of the crib, it is time to stop using it.

Playpens

You can avoid playpen accidents by being aware of the regulations for design, construction, and performance of playpens under Canada's *Hazardous Products Act.* It is illegal to sell a playpen, new or used, that does not meet the following specifications.

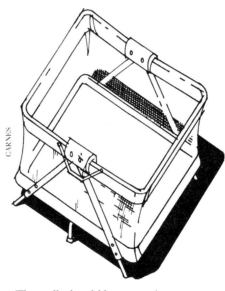

- The walls should be mosquito-type netting to prevent clothing, buttons, or hooks from getting caught.
- To reduce their movement, playpens should not have more than two wheels or casters.
- All playpens should be stable and sturdy, with walls at least 48 cm (19 in.) high.
- All parts must be free from rough or sharp edges. Hinges should be designed to prevent pinching or accidental collapse.
- To prevent finger entrapment, any open holes drilled in metal, plastic, or wood components should be less than

3 mm (1/8 in.) or more than 10 mm (3/8 in.) in diameter.
- All parts that are small enough for a child to choke on must be firmly attached.
- Vinyl rails and mattress pads should not be torn. A child may bite off small pieces and choke.
- An infant should not be left in a drop-sided mesh playpen when one of the sides is not fixed firmly in the fully raised position. The infant may become entrapped and suffocate in the space created between the floor pad and the loose mesh side.
- Don't put scarves, necklaces, long cords, or large toys in a playpen or crib.

Strollers

Strollers provide you with an opportunity to get some exercise, while showing your baby the sights and sounds of the world. Federal regulations governing strollers were passed in 1985. Accidents can be prevented if:
- the restraining straps are always used to prevent the child from falling forward and tipping the stroller over or setting it in motion,
- care is taken to prevent injury to fingers when folding and unfolding strollers, and when reversing the handle on reversible handle strollers,
- heavy packages that could upset the stroller's balance are carried another way or at another time,
- the stroller is checked regularly for dangers such as sharp edges, tears in the upholstery, malfunctioning brakes, or loose wheels,
- older models are checked to make sure they don't collapse when the baby is in them, and
- the instructions that accompany new strollers and carriages are read carefully.

Walkers

Walkers are unnecessary baby equipment and are not recommended. They allow babies to move very quickly into danger zones. Babies may be injured by bumping into furniture, pulling on dangling iron cords or tablecloths (resulting in burns and bruises), falling down stairs (resulting in head injuries or broken bones), or simply falling over. Walkers can provide quick access to poisonous plants, cigarette butts on coffee tables, or medications left on night tables. Moreover, walkers do not help babies to learn to walk. In some cases, they may even delay walking. If you do decide to purchase a walker, consider the following precautions.

- Choose a walker with a wide base that doesn't collapse easily, does not fit through a door, and has a lap belt.
- Look for a walker that complies with the Canadian Juvenile Products Association voluntary standard (indicated on the label).
- Never leave your child alone in the walker.
- Be sure all dangerous items are secured (stairs, cords, tablecloths, poisons, etc.).
- Limit the time your baby spends in a walker to 30 minutes per day.

Baby Gates

In 1990, new regulations were introduced under the *Hazardous Products Act* to prohibit the sale of accordion-style baby gates. The banned gates, made of wood or hard plastic, have large V-shaped openings along the top and/or diamond shaped openings along the sides. These openings are large enough for a baby's head to enter and become entrapped. When choosing a gate, keep in mind where you might be using it and whether you will be able to secure it firmly. Gates with a pressure bar should be placed with the bar side away from the child.

Infant Carriers

Be careful when using infant carriers, they can be dangerous.

Things to remember:
- Never leave your child alone, even when it seems safe.
- The carrier should have a wide solid base, so it can't tip over.
- If a seat has wire supports that snap on the back, make sure they are secure.
- If it has a handle, make sure the locking device is working well.
- Fasten straps and restraining buckles every time you use the seat. They should be adjusted to fit comfortably and to prevent your baby from turning in the seat.
- **Important:** A baby carrier is *not* a car seat and must never be used as one.

Babies in infant carriers should not be placed on tables, especially active babies over two months of age. An active baby may lunge forward, tip the recliner, and fall to the floor causing a head injury.

CHAPMAN

After Pregnancy

Not surprisingly, having been pregnant for nine months, it takes your body a while to return to its pre-pregnant state following childbirth. The weight you gained during pregnancy does not all disappear once the baby is born (remember to continue pre-natal exercises, see p. 21), nor will menstruation resume again immediately. If you do not breastfeed your baby, menstruation should return within eight weeks after birth. If you do breastfeed, menstruation will likely not occur until you stop, although this is not a certainty. There are a number of other things you may experience as your body returns to its pre-pregnant state.

Afterpain

After delivery, the uterus contracts and descends into the pelvic area. You may not feel these contractions with the birth of your first baby. They may be painful, however, if you have had previous births. The pain is due to repeated stretching of the uterine muscles, which have lost some of their elasticity.

Afterpains are often felt most strongly during breastfeeding, as the baby's sucking promotes uterine contractions. Breathing and relaxation techniques that were helpful during pregnancy may help. If the pains persist, a mild pain-relieving drug may be prescribed by the doctor. Afterpains usually disappear after the first week.

Lochia (Flow)

Following the baby's birth, whether vaginal or Caesarean, there will be bleeding and discharge from the vagina for a period of two to six weeks. This is caused by the uterus shedding and renewing its lining. Over the first two to three days, this flow is dark with clots and has a non-offensive odour. It then lessens and becomes brownish, similar to what you experience during the last days of a menstrual period. After the tenth day, the discharge is yellowish white. You should call the doctor or nurse if your flow differs very much from that described.

The nurses in the hospital will teach you how to give yourself "pericare" — careful cleansing of the perineum to prevent infection and odour. Pericare promotes healing and comfort if you have had a vaginal tear or an episiotomy.

Lost Urination Sensation

The nerves to the uterus, bladder, and lower intestine are closely linked. Consequently, they are affected by the stretching in this area during birth. So, for a short time after birth, you may lose the sensation that your bladder is full. For this reason, the nurse may ask you to urinate at regular intervals, whether you think you must go or not. This prevents the bladder from becoming too full. The sensation returns to the bladder in one to two days.

Difficult Bowel Movements

Most mothers have a bowel movement by the third day after birth. To make bowel elimination less difficult, your diet should include naturally laxative foods such as whole grains, bran, dried fruits (especially prunes and figs), fresh fruits, vegetables, and juices. It is important to drink plenty of fluids as well.

If you have had an episiotomy, you may find that supporting the incision with a cool, clean, wet pad is comforting when you have your first bowel movement. Some mothers find that they require the aid of a laxative or enema in re-establishing regular bowel habits. This would be ordered by the doctor.

Hemorrhoids

Hemorrhoids can be a bother after birth as well as during pregnancy. You can obtain relief by avoiding standing for long periods and keeping bowel movements soft to avoid straining when going to the bathroom. Using special pads and ointments and taking sitz baths with Epsom salts will also bring relief.

Menstruation

Menstruation will probably not occur as long as your baby's sole source of nourishment is breastfeeding. If you do not breastfeed your baby, menstruation should return within eight weeks after the birth.

Pregnancy can occur before menstruation recurs. Therefore, it is necessary to use some form of contraception to avoid pregnancy even before menstruation returns (see the Pregnancy Prevention chart on p. 109 in this handbook).

Am I Blue?

Baby Blues

Within the first three to five days after delivery, up to 80 per cent of mothers feel temporary emotional distress referred to as the "postpartum blues." If you are one of these women, you could find yourself feeling restless, irritable, tearful, discouraged, depressed, or helpless. This depressed mood might then be replaced abruptly by a sense of elation. You could feel suddenly energetic and talkative. No treatment is necessary for the baby blues since the experience comes to an end spontaneously.

There are both physical and emotional reasons for the mood swings. Sudden drops in estrogen and progesterone levels tend to be contributing factors. (You might even have experienced similar moods to a lesser degree in the past, at the beginning of your menstrual periods.) Also, you may find the hospital environment stressful. After all, the hospital staff and routines are unfamiliar. Being alone in a room or amongst strangers can produce uneasiness. Where rooming-in (keeping your baby with you) is not available, some mothers feel anxious about being unable to see their baby when they want to.

CHAPMAN

Postpartum Depression

Some women will experience postpartum depression following the birth of their babies. This can occur at any time following the birth. All women experiencing postpartum depression feel disabled by it. Postpartum depression may be characterized by:
- tearfulness,
- despondency,
- feelings of inadequacy and inability to cope,
- alterations of sleep patterns,
- loss of appetite,
- feelings of isolation and worthlessness,
- loss of interest in sexual relations, or
- feelings of exhaustion.

Women with postpartum depression may also experience some of the following:
- a sense of unreality,
- a tangled web of feelings: one minute feeling excited and elated, the next feeling depressed and tearful,
- confusion resulting from transition from a full-functioning, independent person to somebody's mom,
- overwhelming feelings of responsibility, or
- the feeling that motherhood is not as rosy and glowing as expected.

If you feel like crying during this period you should do so unashamedly, as this may give you some relief. It also helps to talk about these feelings with someone.

If these feelings persist for more than a few days, you should contact your doctor, public health nurse, or the nearest postpartum support group. For more information on where to get help, see the article "A Guide to Further Resources" at the back of this handbook.

Questions Often Asked about Breastfeeding

I f you have questions about breastfeeding that aren't answered below, contact your local health unit to speak with a public health nurse or nutritionist, or call your family doctor.

There are times my baby wants to breastfeed more often. Do I have enough milk?

Breastfed babies do feed often. Human milk is easier to digest than formula. Feed your baby frequently. This feeding helps the milk supply. Most women are able to make more than enough milk to satisfy their babies.

How can I tell if my baby is getting enough?

Your baby is getting enough breast milk if your baby is content after most feedings and feeds eight to ten times a day for the first two or three weeks. Babies will have at least two dirty diapers a day for the first few weeks (a breastfed baby's stools may be a mustard coloured, seedy stain about the size of two loonies). Breastfed babies gain an average of 120 to 210 g (4 to 7 oz.) per week for the first four to five months.

Your baby will have growth spurts and may feed often for several days. The more you breastfeed, the more milk your body makes, so you don't need to supplement with formula. Check your baby's weight gain regularly at your health unit or doctor's office.

I thought I wanted to breastfeed but I am feeling frustrated and want to quit. What should I do?

A newborn baby is an overwhelming and exhausting responsibility. But this is a very short time in your life. When you feel frustrated or overwhelmed, call your support person to talk about it. Once you and your baby get to know each other you will find breastfeeding one of the most rewarding parts of caring for your baby.

My milk looks thin and watery. Is it all right?

Yes, your milk is fine. You will notice that your milk changes as your baby is feeding at each breast. At the beginning of a feed on one breast, your milk will look thin and bluish. This will be followed by richer, creamier milk at the end of the feed on that breast.

My "let down" does not happen easily. What can I do?

"Let down" usually happens when your baby suckles or cries. Your body "lets down" the milk to the nipple. If you are tense or anxious or stressed your milk may not let down or it may be delayed. If this happens, try to find a quiet spot away from distractions, apply moist heat to your breast (a warm washcloth may help), make yourself comfortable and try to relax. See "Learning How to Breastfeed" (p. 69) and "Expressing and Storing Breast Milk" (p. 86). Some women don't feel the prickly sensation of "let down." If your baby feeds contentedly and is gaining weight, you might be a woman who doesn't feel "let down."

My breasts don't feel full and they seem smaller. Have I lost my milk?

No, you have not lost your milk. Once you have been breastfeeding for a few weeks, your breasts become more like your normal size. This is because your milk production has adjusted to your baby's needs, and the initial fullness has gone down.

My nipples are sore. What can I do?

Breastfeeding shouldn't hurt. There are a number of things you can do to help sore nipples:

- Try different breastfeeding positions and make sure your baby's mouth is correctly latched on your breast (see "Learning How to Breastfeed" on p. 69).
- Feed your baby more often (at least every two to three hours) and for shorter periods.
- Begin breastfeeding with the less sore side.
- Do not wash nipples after breastfeeding.
- Avoid using soap on your nipples.
- Try exposing your nipples to air.
- Make sure your nursing bra is not tight. Use cotton breast pads and change them when they are damp.
- If it's a continuing problem, see your doctor and check out the possibility of an infection.

CALDWELL

My breasts are engorged — heavy, full of milk, and painful. How can I get relief from this?

Engorgement can happen when your milk first comes in *or* when you miss a feeding. In either case, feeding your baby frequently, at least every two to three hours will help. If you make a lot of milk, use one breast at each feeding so your baby drains that side before going on to the second side.

If your breast is red and painful, apply moist heat and drain it by feeding baby on that side. It may help to take a warm shower, firmly massage your breasts, and express some milk. This will make your breasts feel more comfortable and soften them so your baby can feed properly. Try not to skip a feeding without expressing your milk. You may need to pump your breasts to help empty them after a feed. If the redness or pain continues, see your doctor. (See "Expressing and Storing Breast Milk" on p. 86.)

I have a small lumpy area on one breast. It is red and hot to the touch. What is wrong?

You could be suffering from one of two conditions — a plugged duct or a breast infection (mastitis).

A plugged duct usually happens when the duct is not regularly or fully emptied. Plugged ducts can become infected. You can relieve plugged ducts by:

• Breastfeeding your baby more often. The sucking will help loosen the clogged milk. This milk is still fresh and fine for your baby to drink. Try to keep the breast as empty as possible. Do this by letting your baby suck on the sore breast first, or express milk by hand.

• Have your baby's chin close to the sore spot for the strongest possible sucking action.

• Use a warm, wet washcloth or your fingers to massage the lump toward the nipple while your baby is feeding on the breast. This aids proper drainage.

• If your nipple is covered by any dried secretions, take a warm shower before breastfeeding or soak your breast in warm water for five to ten minutes.

• Use moist heat to make yourself more comfortable. It will also promote drainage between feedings.

• Make sure your bra and clothing are comfortable, not too tight.

• Don't lie in positions that put pressure on one spot for a long time.

• Get plenty of rest, eat a variety of foods from the "Food Guide for Pregnancy and Breastfeeding" on p. 16, and remember to drink plenty of fluids.

If you develop a temperature, or if the lump lasts, you may have mastitis. Mastitis may also make you feel sick, causing chills and aches. If you think you have mastitis, call your doctor immediately. Mastitis can be treated with antibiotics and possibly pain relievers. In most cases, *women with a breast infection should continue to breastfeed.* It will not make your baby sick. However, feed more often and start on the sore breast to empty it first.

Milk leaks from my breasts even when I'm not feeding my baby. What can I do?

This is common in the first few weeks of breastfeeding. You can stop the leaking by applying pressure with the palm of your hand until the leaking stops. Wear cotton pads inside your bra. Change them when they become damp to protect your nipples from infection.

Can I breastfeed my baby if I am sick?

Yes. If you have a cold or the flu your baby has already been exposed to it by the time you feel sick. Antibodies in your milk protect your baby.

Do I have to stop eating spicy foods while I breastfeed?

No. Most babies do well whatever their mothers eat. If you notice that a particular food seems to cause your baby problems you can stop eating that one. Sometimes your baby's upset is only a coincidence, so try the food again and see what happens. It's important that you continue to eat and enjoy a variety of foods from the "Food Guide for Pregnancy and Breastfeeding" on p. 16.

My baby is gassy. What should I do?

You don't have to do anything. Most babies pass gas. It doesn't mean your baby's stomach is upset or that your baby needs burping.

Can I diet while I'm breastfeeding?

No. Dieting isn't recommended. Your body needs to recover from pregnancy. See "What Should I Eat When I'm Breastfeeding?" on p. 71.

Can I give my baby a bottle occasionally?

Yes. Once you have settled into a breastfeeding routine (after four to six weeks, usually) you can introduce an occasional cup or bottle of breast milk. Remember to empty your breast when you get home if you have missed a feed. This milk can be stored for future use.

Expressing and Storing Breast Milk

When you breastfeed and need to be away at feeding time, you can express milk ahead of time and store it for someone else to feed to your baby in a cup or bottle. Breast milk can be expressed by hand or with an electric or manual breast pump. You can express breast milk any time. Do not worry if you only collect a small amount the first few times you pump. Breast milk should not be boiled or pasteurized when you store it for your baby. That would decrease its special nutritional and health protection value.

It is easiest to express breast milk in the morning, about an hour after your baby has fed. Or you can breastfeed your baby at one breast and express at the other. The amount of milk you will be able to express will range from a few drops to a few ounces. It will vary at different times of day and for different mothers.

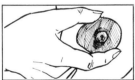

BURGESS

To Express Milk by Hand

- Wash your hands with soap and water.
- Have a clean cup, bowl, or jar ready to catch the milk.
- Get comfortable.
- Massage your breast in a circular motion working from shoulder to nipple.
- To start milk "let down," brush your hand across the nipple or roll it between your thumb and finger.
- Put your hand in a C-shape on your breast. Put fingers on the bottom and your thumb on the top at the outer edge of the areola.
- Press straight back into the breast towards your chest. If your breast is larger, lift it before pressing inward.
- Gently squeeze your thumb and fingers together while you move them towards the nipple, but do not pinch your nipple.
- Catch the milk in the clean cup, bowl, or jar.
- Move your fingers around the areola in a circle to express

from different parts of your breast.
- Express until the milk stops.
- Switch to the other breast.
- You may need to repeat this procedure more than once each time you express milk.

Once you learn how, it is easy to do!

Some women prefer to use a manual or electric breast pump. Always follow the instructions that come with the pump. Follow all directions for cleaning. *Do not use manual breast pumps with rubber bulbs. They can hurt your nipples.*

Seeing expressed breast milk may surprise you. Breast milk is usually watery and bluish white. What you eat may change the colour of your breast milk, but your baby will like it just as well.

To Store Breast Milk

Breast milk should be stored in single-feeding amounts. It may take several collections to get enough for one feeding. Baby-bottle liners, clean plastic baby bottles, and plastic freezer bags are convenient storage containers. Close the container tightly, remove as much air as you can, and label with the date.

Store your expressed breast milk for no more than three days in the fridge, two weeks in the freezer compartment of a one-door fridge, three months in the freezer of a two-door fridge, or six months in a deep freeze.

To collect enough for one feeding, you can cool your milk in the fridge and then add it to already frozen milk.

Thawing and Warming Breast Milk

Always use the oldest milk first. Breast milk often separates when it is frozen. Just shake it gently to remix it once it thaws.

Thaw breast milk by putting the container in the fridge or under cold running water until thawed. *Never thaw breast milk at room temperature or in the microwave. Milk should never be refrozen.* Milk that has been frozen and then kept at room temperature or heated is no longer safe for your baby to drink and should be discarded. (Heating on top of the stove destroys valuable nutrients and protective factors of breast milk.)

Warm breast milk by putting it under warm running tap water or in a container of warm water.

For more information on expressing and storing breast milk or on where to find breast pumps, call your public health nurse or lactation consultant, or La Leche League.

Microwave Safety

It is not safe to use the microwave oven to thaw or warm breast milk or formula. The microwave also destroys valuable nutrients and protective factors of breast milk. Heating is uneven, so there is a danger of hot spots which can scald baby's mouth. Glass bottles with caps on can explode. Plastic bottles, bags, and containers can decompose in the microwave.

Bottlefeeding Your Baby

Feeding young babies is important for two reasons. It gives them the food they need, while holding and cuddling them helps them to bond. Both are necessary for babies to grow well and be healthy.

Babies should be fed when they are hungry. This is called "feeding on demand." Babies know when they are hungry and how much they need. A baby's needs can change from day to day. A parent's job is to provide the food when the baby needs it. This is true for breastfed and formula fed babies.

If you are bottlefeeding, the next best food after breast milk is commercial infant formula. Feed only breast milk, infant formula, or water from a bottle. Do not feed juice, tea, baby cereal, or pop from bottles. See "Baby's First Foods" (p. 92) for starting juice in a cup and cereal with a spoon.

Make sure you choose a commercial formula that is meant for newborn babies, not one of the "follow up" formulas for older babies.

Give commercial infant formula until your baby is 9 to 12 months old. If you find you cannot afford commercial formula when your baby is very young, talk to your public health nurse or nutritionist about restarting your own milk. They may help you access formula or tell you how to make evaporated milk formula — the only choice *after* commercial formula.

Do not give ordinary cow's milk, goat's milk, or soy milk to babies younger than 9 to 12 months. These are not breast milk substitutes. These milks can hurt your baby's stomach and kidneys.

Infant formula comes in three forms:
- **Powdered** (you add water),
- **Concentrated** (you add an equal amount of water), or
- **Ready-to-serve** (no water needs to be added).

Compare costs. Powdered formula usually costs the least; ready-to-serve costs the most. The cost of preparing a bottle from concentrate is often about the same as from powder.

Steps for Safe Bottlefeeding

- Choose the formula you will use. If you do not have a fridge, choose powdered formula and make up only one bottle at the time you feed your baby.
- Check the tin for an expiry date. Do not buy formula if the date is past.
- Learn the right amount of water to add to the formula you're making. Make only one day's supply at a time.
- Wash your hands with soap and water.
- Clean and sterilize bottles, nipples, rings, and caps. (This can be done ahead of time.) If you use bottles with plastic liners, you only need to sterilize the nipples and wash the holders. The liners are clean and ready to use.
- Wash bottle parts well in hot, soapy water and pay special attention to the insides of bottles and nipples.
- Rinse them well.
- Sterilize by boiling in a clean, uncovered pot for five minutes. Also sterilize the mixing container and mixing spoon.
- Remove bottle parts from water and fit nipples, caps, and rings together with nipple on the inside of the bottle.
- Store bottles until you need to fill them with formula.
- Boil the water that you need in a pot (not a tea kettle) for five minutes and cool it with the lid on. In most cases, you can stop boiling the water and sterilizing the bottles after your baby is three months old. If you have concerns about your water supply or if you have a well, check with your health unit about using this water for your baby.
- Mix the formula — it's important to your baby's health to have the right amount of water for the amount of powder or liquid used.
- If you are using powdered formula, check the directions on the label for mixing. Be sure to use the measure in the can and the number of scoops recommended for each bottle of formula.
- Measure into a clean container the amount of boiled water you need for the number of bottles you are making (make only one day's supply of formula at a time).
- Add the powder or liquid concentrate and mix gently.
- Pour the formula into the bottles and cap them.
- Store prepared formula in the fridge.
- Any formula left at the end of 24 hours must *not* be given to your baby. Leftover formula from your baby's feeds may be used for adults or cooking, but not saved for your baby.
- Store opened cans of concentrate and ready-to-serve

formula in the fridge. Make sure cans are covered. Discard opened cans of liquid formula after two days.

• Store powdered formula in a cool, dry place (not in the fridge). Make sure the lid is tightly closed.

Warming Your Baby's Bottle

• Some babies prefer formula at body temperature, others like it cool. Either way is fine.

• Warm formula by heating the bottle in a bowl or saucepan of hot water. Always test heated milk on your wrist. It should feel just warm.

• Microwaving is *not* recommended. Hot spots in formula can scald babies, glass bottles can explode, and plastic can decompose. Use only microwave-safe glass containers and carefully follow directions for the microwave. (If you do microwave formula or milk, be sure you mix the liquid well and test the temperature before you offer it to your baby.)

Bottlefeeding Tips

• Wash your hands before feeding your baby.

• Get comfortable so you can relax and pay attention to your baby while holding and feeding him or her. (Some babies and parents are bothered when they have company at feeding time.)

• Don't rush. Each baby's rhythm for eating is different and you need to respect this. Some babies take half an hour or longer to eat.

• Hold your baby's head higher than his or her body — otherwise it's hard to swallow without choking. (If you try drinking when you are flat on your back you'll see what it's like.)

MASSE

• Hold the bottle so that most of the nipple is in your baby's mouth and the formula fills the nipple. This will prevent your baby from swallowing a lot of air.

• *Never prop the bottle, your baby could choke.*

• Burp your baby gently part way through the feed.

• Learn to tell when your baby has had enough. Let your baby end the feeding. Remove the bottle gently from your baby's mouth.

• Read "Caring for Your Baby's Mouth" on p. 99.

Feeding can be a time of special closeness with your baby — enjoy!

Extra Vitamins and Minerals — Does Your Baby Need Them?

Breastfed babies receive all the necessary nutrients in adequate amounts, except vitamin D. Since infants and children under two years of age require 10 micrograms (400 I.U.) of vitamin D every day, a supplement should be started at birth and continued until your child is drinking two cups of whole cow's milk each day.

Bottlefed babies will likely not need a vitamin supplement, because commercial formulas are fortified with vitamins and minerals. However, it is a good idea to confirm this with your doctor or public health nurse. Some parents wonder if they should give their baby formula with iron. Check with your doctor to decide if your baby needs formula with iron before you buy this type of formula. Formula-fed babies need iron rich foods such as infant cereal from four months of age. Breastfed babies need no solid foods before six months (see "Baby's First Foods" on page 92). It is most important that babies who are not breastfed be given formula, *not regular cow's milk*, until nine months of age.

If you have a premature or low birth-weight baby, check with your doctor about any special vitamin or mineral requirements.

Why Is the Baby Crying?

There is nothing like a crying baby to make parents feel helpless, guilty, even angry. But difficult though the crying may be to deal with at times, it is your baby's only way of letting you know that he or she is unhappy about something. If babies are tired, sick, hungry, frustrated, wet, or just plain lonely, they say so by crying.

Many newborns, when they aren't eating or sleeping, spend a great deal of time crying. When this happens, it is best to stay relaxed and move slowly and calmly around and with your baby.

If you've ruled out hunger as a reason for the crying, ask yourself if the baby is overdressed, underdressed, sick, or bored. Does he or she have diaper rash or indigestion, need cuddling or attention? Often, your baby will just be tired and is crying as a means of self-comfort. If that's the case, you might try putting the baby to bed and allow him or her to cry for a while to settle down. It might be a good idea to set a timer for five to fifteen minutes. Otherwise, this settling-down period will seem like an eternity.

Staying cool is often easier said than done, especially if the baby's crying goes on for a long time. Feeling frustrated is a natural response. It's important to recognize, though, that allowing anger to overwhelm you will probably only make the baby cry more.

Above all, remember that babies are fragile beings, easily harmed. Never handle a baby roughly, no matter how provoked. Shaking or throwing a small child can cause whiplash or bleeding. It can even bruise the infant's brain. Paralysis, lifelong mental impairment, or even death could be the result. If you feel in danger of losing your temper and harming your baby in this way, make it your first priority to find some way of letting off steam and regaining composure. If necessary, just leave the room or call on another adult for help.

No matter how puzzling or frustrating your baby's crying may seem at first, you will soon learn to understand the reason(s) for the tears and how best to respond. In the meantime, you can check this chart for ideas on why your baby is crying and what you can do about it.

Reason for crying	What you can do about it
Hungry or thirsty	• Feed the baby, especially if it is more than two hours since the last feeding. (Remember, though, that overfeeding can cause colic.)
Uncomfortable	• Burp the baby. • Check diaper pins. • Change the diaper if it is wet or soiled. • Change the baby's position. • Give the baby a gentle back rub. • Check the room temperature to make sure it isn't too warm or too cold. • Check clothes and covers to make sure the baby isn't overdressed or underdressed.
Insecure	• Wrap the baby snugly in a light blanket. • Create a secure environment by moving slowly and calmly (avoid rushed or jerky movements). • Hold the baby close to your body and cuddle.
Lonely or bored	• Talk or sing to your baby. • Take baby into a room with others. • Turn on the TV or play soothing music. • Rock the baby. • Take the baby for a walk. • Have an interesting toy or mobile for the baby to watch. • Smile at the baby and establish eye contact.

FEDORUK

Reason for crying	What you can do about it
Overstimulated or overtired	• Move to quieter surroundings (e.g., place the baby on his or her tummy on a plain white sheet). • Offer breast or pacifier. • Try a quiet, rhythmic motion (e.g., rocking, patting, going for a carriage or car ride). • Create a soothing background by turning on the dishwasher, clothes dryer, or vacuum cleaner (many babies like sounds of this sort, which may actually remind them of the sound of mother's heartbeat and blood circulation before birth). • Take a warm bath with the baby. • Listen carefully to the sounds your baby makes — you will soon discover what your baby's needs are. Remember, it is normal for babies to move and make sounds, even when sleeping. It can be disturbing to them to be picked up unnecessarily.
Fussy time of day (usually late afternoon or evening)	• Try previous suggestions, if appropriate. • Reduce household tension (e.g., prepare supper ahead of time, have activities planned for other children). • Have your partner, a grandparent, or some other person available to spend time with the baby or to free you up so you can be with the baby.

Some parents are afraid that if they give too much attention, they will spoil their baby. Nothing could be further from the truth. Babies need attention, cuddling, and handling. When babies cry, they need more care, not less. They just have no other way of telling you they need something. The best thing to do is to pick up and cuddle your baby. In discovering what your baby needs, your own loving instincts and feelings will be the very best guide of all.

What Is Colic?

Colic is best described as a sudden abdominal pain that comes and goes, often during the evening. The baby's tummy feels hard, and he or she draws the knees up to the tummy and cries. Colic generally begins after the second or third week of life and lasts until the third or fourth month. It usually stops quite suddenly. No one knows what causes colic, or why healthy babies who are growing well have it.

For the most part, there is not much that can be done about colic other than making sure the baby burps after meals, is kept warm and quiet, and is given plenty of love and cuddling. See the article "Why Is the Baby Crying" (p. 89) for more suggestions. If none of these helps check with your doctor to ensure your baby is well.

It can be difficult to remain calm while caring for a colicky baby. You will find that leaving baby with a trustworthy sitter and going out for an evening once in a while is a much-needed help.

We don't have simple answers or solutions to colic. Some books and a video that may assist you are:
• Books: *The Fussy Baby* by William Sears, M.D., and *Curing Infant Colic* by Bruce Taubman, M.D.
• Video: "Infant Crying: The First Six Months" produced by Williams and Ledger, Ltd.
If you require further assistance or advice, check with your doctor or public health nurse.

Babies and Allergies

Breastfeeding is the best way to prevent cow's-milk allergies in babies. Babies from families with allergies are more likely to have allergies themselves. For these babies, avoid *any* exposure to cow's milk or cow's-milk formula in the first six months.

Allergic symptoms in babies with food allergies may include stomach pains, diarrhea, vomiting or frequent spitting up, skin rashes or eczema, or constant runny nose. These symptoms may have other causes. If your baby frequently has any of these symptoms, talk them over with your public health nurse or doctor. If baby appears to have an allergy, ask for a referral to an allergy specialist (a dietitian, nutritionist, or doctor). These specialists can help you find the safest choices for feeding your baby. If you are breastfeeding, this may mean changing your own food choices.

Removing a major food or a whole food group requires careful planning and consultation with a dietitian or nutritionist in order to meet the nutrition needs of you and your baby. When introducing solid foods, follow the guidelines in "Baby's First Foods" on p. 92. After introducing any new food, wait three to five days before introducing another. This gives you time to learn if a certain food causes a reaction in your baby.

Ask at your health unit for more information on food allergies.

Weaning Your Baby from the Breast

The decision about when to wean your baby will depend on the baby's readiness, your family circumstances, and your own preferences. The Canadian Pediatric Society recommends that infants be breastfed into the second year of life.

Weaning should be gradual:
• You can eliminate one breastfeeding a day. To start, choose a time when your baby is least hungry or when you are most likely to be away. A commercial infant formula could

CALDWELL.

be substituted for this feeding, or you could offer the baby whole cow's milk if your baby is older than 9 to 12 months and is eating a variety of foods each day.

- When you and your baby are ready, another breastfeeding can be left out, again substituting formula or whole cow's milk.
- Check "Baby's First Foods" (below) for the total amount of formula or milk your baby needs.
- Some breastfed older babies are used to nursing frequently for comfort, so you may not need to give milk in a cup or bottle to replace every feeding you eliminate. Your baby's behaviour will be your guide.
- Reduce breastfeeding gradually to one feeding a day. You can then nurse just enough to relieve the fullness you feel in your breasts.
- After a week of one feeding a day, you can skip days and nurse only when your breasts are too full to be comfortable. By this time, your milk production will be very low and will eventually stop.
- Babies usually accept weaning better if they are not rushed.
- If your baby is teething or not feeling well, you may wish to delay weaning.
- When weaning, check your breasts daily for lumps and soreness. If lumps appear, massage your breasts in a warm shower or with a warm, wet washcloth to help unblock the milk ducts.
- Check with a public health nurse or doctor if you have any difficulties.

Baby's First Foods

When Do I Start Other Food?

- When your baby is ready, which is usually around four to six months of age.

What Do I Start With?

- Begin with iron-fortified, single-grain, commercial infant cereals.
- Later add plain foods, with no added sugar, salt, or fat.

How Do I Start?

- Offer one new food at a time.
- Wait at least three days before giving your baby another new food.

How Much Does Baby Need?

- Babies will shut their mouths, turn their heads, and push food away when they have had enough to eat. Watch for these signs when feeding.

- The amounts of food listed are only general guides. It is fine for your baby to eat more or less, as he or she chooses.

What About Cow's Milk?

- Breast milk is the best milk for your baby. Commercial formula is the next best.
- Wait until your baby is at least 9 to 12 months old and eating regular meals of family foods before offering drinks of whole milk once in a while.
- Choose whole (homogenized) milk and be sure it is pasteurized.
- Babies need more fat than adults, so use whole milk until age two.
- Lower-fat milks can be given after age two.
- Soy "milk," rice "milk," and nut "milk" should not be used instead of cow's milk.

Tips for Happy Mealtimes

To help your baby develop healthy food habits and happy, relaxed feelings about eating:

- Let your baby decide how much and whether to eat. (You choose when and what food will be offered.)
- Remember — messiness is a normal part of learning to eat.
- Offer finger foods and foods with more texture between six and nine months. They allow your baby to develop important feeding skills.

Safety Tips

- Honey could cause infant botulism and is not recommended for infants under one year.
- Some foods aren't safe for babies because they can cause choking. Some of these are: popcorn, seeds, nuts, hard or chewy candies, and hard, raw vegetables. Wieners and grapes should be sliced lengthwise. Always be with your baby while he or she is eating.

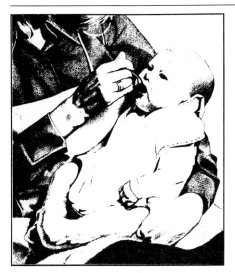

FOUR TO SIX MONTHS

Four to Six Months

- Breast milk on demand, or formula — 1000 to 1250 mL (32 to 40 oz.) daily.

Feed solids one to two times per day.

- Begin with iron-fortified infant cereal mixed with breast milk, water, or formula. Start with 5 mL (1 tsp.) and increase to 60 mL (4 tbsp.) daily.

- After a month or so, baby may enjoy well mashed vegetables and fruit, such as banana, cooked sweet potato, squash, potato, peaches, pears, and applesauce (canned without sugar). Start with 5 mL (1 tsp.) and increase to 60 mL (4 tbsp.) daily. (Note: If your baby needs *puréed* fruits and vegetables, then he or she is not ready for these foods.)

- Breast milk is the best food for the first four to six months. After you start solids, it is still important to continue breastfeeding as much as you can. Commercial formula is the next best choice after breast milk.

Six to Nine Months

- Breast milk on demand, or formula — 750 to 1000 mL (24 to 32 oz.) daily.

Feed solids three to four times per day.

- Infant cereal — 60 to 125 mL (4 to 8 tbsp.) daily.

- Vegetables and fruit (mashed) — 60 to 125 mL (4 to 8 tbsp.) daily and unsweetened juice offered in a cup — up to 50 mL (1/4 cup) daily.

- Try adding ground up meat, fish, or poultry; cooked, mashed, dried beans, lentils, egg yolk, tofu, cottage cheese, or plain yogurt. Start with 5 mL (1 tsp.) and increase to 100 mL (6 tbsp.) daily.

- Later you can try finger foods: pieces of peeled fruit (peach, pear, orange, bananas, kiwi, plums, melon), soft cooked vegetables (carrot, broccoli, cauliflower, potato), toast, squares of bread, crackers, cooked pasta, "oat rings" cereal, and pieces of soft cheese.

- *Avoid* small pieces that may cause choking, such as nuts, seeds, raw peas, raw carrots, corn, popcorn, wieners, grapes.

- Babies can enjoy mashed foods and finger foods before teeth appear.

- At first, babies may do more playing with finger foods than eating. That is how they learn. Finger foods are fun!

SIX TO NINE MONTHS

NINE TO TWELVE MONTHS

Nine to Twelve Months

- Breast milk on demand, or formula — 625 to 950 mL (20 to 30 oz.) daily. (Milk requirements will decrease as a baby eats more solids.)

Feed solids four to six times per day.

- Infant cereal — 60 to 125 mL (4 to 8 tbsp.) daily.

- Vegetables and fruit (small soft pieces) — 125 to 250 mL (1/2 to 1 cup) daily and unsweetened juice offered in a cup — up to 125 mL (1/2 cup) daily.

- Meat, fish, poultry, cooked dried beans (ground or chopped), lentils, egg yolk, tofu, cottage cheese, or plain yogurt — 75 to 125 mL (1/3 to 1/2 cup) daily.

- Finger foods.

- Add egg white towards the end of the first year.

- Whole milk can be given occasionally once your baby is eating regular meals and a variety of solid foods.

- By one year, your baby should be eating table foods and enjoying family mealtime.

- Learning to eat takes time and patience. Expect some mess and relax.

Preparing Baby's Food

Keep it plain and simple:
- Your baby's first food can easily be plain, healthy family food, mashed or ground to a texture your baby will enjoy.

- When you wait until your baby is five to six months old to offer solids other than cereal, there is little need for purées, blenders, or complicated preparation methods.

- Use a potato masher, fork, or food grinder to mash cooked vegetables and fruit. Add a little fruit juice, vegetable liquid, or water to moisten if necessary.

- Manual baby-food grinders are very useful for soft meats, stews, casseroles, and thick home-made soups. Babies enjoy these foods. Just be sure that you have introduced all the ingredients separately to your baby before offering a mixture.

Choosing and Cooking the Best Foods for Your Baby and Your Family

- Choose fresh, high-quality vegetables without blemishes or wilted parts and plain, frozen vegetables without added sauce.

- Choose fully ripe, fresh fruit and canned fruits packed in water or in their own juice.

- Choose lean cuts of meat, fish, and poultry.

- Choose well-cooked or canned dried beans, peas, and lentils.

- Wash your hands before handling food. Utensils and containers should also be very clean.

- Wash vegetables and fruit thoroughly.

- Steam or microwave fresh or frozen vegetables until tender-crisp.

- Bake, stew, or broil meats when possible.

- Remove baby's portion before seasoning with salt or sugar.

Storing Baby's Food

- Baby's foods should be covered and refrigerated immediately.

- Store food in the refrigerator for *no more than three days*, in tightly covered containers. Feeding from the container is not recommended because saliva left from the spoon will introduce germs and can make the food unsafe to eat.

- Freeze tiny portions of leftover stews, home-made soups, meatballs, and casseroles for instant baby meals at a later time.

Thawing and Warming Baby's Food

- Frozen food can be defrosted in the refrigerator or microwave oven.

- Food should never be thawed and refrozen.

Stove Method

- To warm, place food directly in a saucepan and slowly warm over low heat, stirring often. Be sure food is not too hot before offering it to your baby.

Microwave Method

- Heat food in a microwave-safe dish or an opened baby-food jar.

- Cover dish with a microwave-safe cover, not plastic wrap.

- Stir food and turn the dish frequently during the heating process.

- Allow food to sit for a few minutes; stir well and test the temperature before serving.

- **Caution:** Microwave ovens heat foods unevenly and may cause hot spots. There may be hot spots even if the food feels cool to you. It is important to stir food well in order to prevent burns to you or your baby.

Babytalk

People need to communicate. Even babies develop messages they know you will understand. Messages are sent through facial expressions, body gestures, and pitch of voice. When your baby cries, you pick up your baby and try to understand what he needs. Is it hunger or discomfort? When he coos again (when he's comfortable) you know you have understood. Communication has taken place.

Parents, often without realizing, try to interpret their babies' noises and gestures — their coos, cries, babbles, and body movements. For example, when your baby starts to fuss and the sounds he makes have an urgency about them. You interpret, "Are you hungry? Shall I feed you?," and when he sees the food and his sounds change from distressful to excited, fast, and impatient, you say, "Oh, you are hungry. O.K., I'm hurrying. It's coming, it's coming." Your speech becomes hurried as well, matching that of your baby's. Your baby's body moves in an attempt to reach out. He gets his food, "mmmm." You say, "Ah, that's better." Your tone shows relief, matching that of your baby's.

By asking your baby questions and commenting on his sounds and behaviour, you are having a real conversation. You match many of his sounds, interpret his noises, and focus on what he is doing, on what he is wanting.

Babies don't understand individual words. They hear a steady stream of sound. The tone of our voice plays a big part in both expressing and interpreting the meaning. For example, you say, "Ohhh, you're sleepy." Your tone is soothing, the message is "go to sleep." "It's *morning time!*" Your tone is lively, the message is "time to get up." "I know you aren't happy, but you'll be fine." The tone is reassuring and calm. Your message is, "You're O.K., things aren't that bad."

Likewise, your baby is able to express his message through intonation. For example, when he says "a-ga" with the right intonation, we can hear that he is saying "All gone." He is able to match our intonation pattern correctly long before he can accurately perceive or produce the individual words. When your baby says "da-*Da?*" with emphasis on *Da*, he is expressing, "Is that you Dad?" "*Da-Da*" — "It *is* you!" "*Da-Da!*" (high pitch) — he expresses surprise or excitement, "Great to see you!" "Da-da" (lower pitch) — he commands "Come and get me!"

In these examples, the child is able to express questions, statements, surprise, and commands through intonation and gesture. Language has started and this all happened during everyday activities. You can help your baby along by talking and by singing while bathing, feeding, housecleaning, and playing.

The following chart will help you measure your baby's progress. If you have any concerns or doubts about your baby's speech development, contact your doctor or local health unit/department to obtain professional help. In particular, have your child's hearing tested if you have to talk loudly or repeat a lot to draw attention. Never wait to get help for your child if you suspect a problem.

Age	Does your child . . .
Birth	• make pleasure sounds? • look at you, look away and then look again, when you are playing with him or her?
0 to 3 months	• smile when he or she sees you? • cry differently for different needs? • repeat the same sounds a lot (cooing, gooing)?
4 to 6 months	• babble with lots of different speech — including "p," "b," and "m" sounds? • let you know (by sound or gesture) when he or she wants you to do something again? • make gurgling sounds when left alone or when playing with you?
7 months to 12 months	• say one or two words (e.g., bye-bye, dada, mama, no), although they may not be clear? • imitate different speech sounds? • babble, using both long and short groups of sounds (e.g., tata, up up, bi bi bi bi)? • use his or her voice to get and keep your attention?

This language development (talking) chart is adapted from the pamphlet "How Does Your Child Hear and Talk?" produced by the PSI Iota XI Sorority and the American Speech-Language-Hearing Foundation. The article is adapted from the book *Talking Together* written by Anne Gardner, 1308 Midden Road, Comox, B.C., V9N 7X6.

You may also want to check out *The First Twelve Months of Life*, by Frank Caplan, *Learning Through Play* by Jean Marzollo and Janice Lloyd, and *The First Three Years of Life* (revised edition) by Burton L. White.

Seeing Is Believing

What does a newborn see? Right from birth, babies can distinguish light and dark, shapes and patterns. When they are quiet and alert, babies can focus on objects 18 to 45 cm (7 to 18 in.) away for very brief periods of time. It is also known that they are strongly attracted to the human face.

You may notice that your baby's eyes "wander" or cross independently at times. This is not uncommon in the first three months. Many babies will do this until they develop proper eye co-ordination. However, a constant "wandering" should not be ignored. Discuss this with your family doctor.

Here are some other important things to remember.
• Vision is learned, not inborn.

• Children with a family history of a lazy or crossed eye are at a higher risk of having an eye problem.
• Early treatment of turned eye or decreased vision is essential for best results. Even babies who can't talk can be examined.
• Examination by an eye doctor by age three is recommended.
  If you have any concerns about your baby's vision, contact your doctor or local health unit/department.

Age	Does your child . . .
Birth	• have pupils that adjust to light in the same manner as an older child's pupils?
0 to 3 months	• respond to light from different directions when his or her position in the crib is changed? • respond to a variety of movements (e.g., a mobile outside and above the crib)? • reach and touch objects within focus (about 20 to 30 cm or 8 to 12 in.)? • follow you with his or her eyes as you walk around the room?
4 to 6 months	• explore many different textures and shapes with his or her fingers? • reach across the crib for various objects, or reach for things when playing with you? (shows development of eye, hand, and foot co-ordination) • grasp small objects set before him or her? (shows development of hand-eye co-ordination)
7 to 12 months	• crawl and explore freely? • play games like "peek-a-boo" and "patty cake"? • reach and touch toys and other objects within his or her surroundings?

This chart was developed by the Vision Advisory Committee, British Columbia Ministry of Health, 1991.

Your Baby's Hearing

Your baby will be able to hear from the moment he or she is born. In fact, babies can hear while still inside the mother's body. They can hear their mother's heartbeat and other internal and external noises. That is probably why newborns respond by calming down or becoming alert when they hear repetitious, droning sounds such as a washing machine or a car motor. A baby will also respond to the human voice, especially the mother's. This is because the mother's voice is the first and most consistently heard voice while the baby is still in the womb. Babies can distinguish between different types of sound. In fact, they respond differently to sounds. For example, a baby may move its arms and legs one way when the mother speaks, and a different way when others speak.

Good hearing is very important for normal development of speech and language. It is also important for healthy emotional make-up. Your baby learns and develops by receiving input through sight, touch, and hearing. The chart below will help you measure your baby's progress. As you have daily contact with your child, you know more about your child's hearing than anyone. If you have any concerns about your baby's hearing, contact your doctor, public health nurse, or audiologist immediately. Your baby's hearing can be tested easily and quickly.

DECOSTE

Age	Does your child . . .		
Birth	• listen to speech?	• startle or cry at noises?	• awaken to loud sounds?
0 to 3 months	• turn to you when you speak? • smile when spoken to?	• stop play and appear to listen to sounds or speech? • seem to recognize your voice and quiet down if crying?	
4 to 6 months	• respond to "no" and his or her name? • respond to changes in your tone of voice? • notice and look around for the source of new sounds?		
7 to 12 months	• turn or look up when you call his or her name? • search or look around when hearing new sounds? • listen when spoken to? • recognize words for common items like "cup," "shoe," etc? • respond to some requests such as "come here" and "want more"?		

This language development (hearing) chart is adapted from the pamphlet "How Does Your Child Hear and Talk?" produced by the PSI Iota XI Sorority and the American Speech-Language-Hearing Foundation.

Immunizing Your Baby

Going to the child health clinic or your doctor for routine immunizations is an important part of keeping your baby healthy. It is extremely important that your baby receive the immunizations recommended in the basic immunization schedule below. Your public health nurse has immunization information she will give you. Record immunizations given in the record of immunization or Child Health Passport (available through your local health unit/department).

In the first 12 to 24 hours after the immunization, your baby may be fussy or have a slight fever. He or she may also have a sore leg for one or two days if the injection has been given in the thigh. Usually, all you need to do is cuddle your baby and place cool cloths on the injection site. If your baby has a fever, a lukewarm bath (sponge or tub) and extra fluids (from breast or bottle) should help. A fever-reducing medication such as acetaminophen can also be used as indicated by the public health nurse, your family doctor, or the pharmacist. Please note that there are different concentrations of acetaminophen products; therefore, you must always read the label before use to find the concentration of medication and instructions for giving the medication. Acetylsalicylic acid (ASA or aspirin) is *not* recommended for children.

For more information on immunization and what to do if your baby has a reaction, ask the public health nurse at your local health unit/department or speak to your doctor.

Recommended Basic Immunization Schedule

	1st visit (2 months of age)	2nd visit (2 months after 1st visit)	3rd visit (2 months after 2nd visit)	4th visit (12 months of age)	5th visit (12 months after 3rd visit)	4-6 years of age*
Diphtheria	•	•	•		•	•
Pertussis	•	•	•		•	•
Tetanus	•	•	•		•	•
Poliomyelitis	•	•	•		•	•
Measles				•		
Mumps				•		
Rubella				•		
Haemophilus Influenzae type b	•	•	•		•	

* booster for school entry

Protect Baby's Teeth Now!

Even though "baby" or first teeth are replaced by permanent teeth, baby's first teeth are very important.
• First teeth make it possible for your child to eat solid foods.
• First teeth play a role in helping your baby learn to speak.
• First teeth aid in jaw development and hold the space for the permanent teeth.

Throughout life, healthy teeth are important to appearance, which in turn is important for the development of a good self-image. By starting good dental-care habits early, you will protect the future health of your child's permanent teeth.

Caring for Your Baby's Mouth

You should start to clean your infant's mouth soon after birth. This will develop the habit for yourself and the baby. Regular mouth care will massage the gums and ease teething discomfort.
• Have the child lie comfortably in your lap. This can be a close time for parent and child.
• Wipe all around your baby's gums with a damp washcloth placed over the index finger.
• Move on to a soft baby toothbrush as teeth appear.
• Use of a toothpaste containing fluoride is recommended as soon as the first tooth appears (see "Flouride" on p. 100).
• Brushing should be done daily using a "pea-sized" amount of toothpaste (see illustration).
• The best time to clean your child's mouth is after the last feeding of the day.
• *Note:* When breastfeeding continues after baby's first teeth appear, regular cleaning of the teeth is necessary.

Hidden Dangers

First teeth are very susceptible to decay, which can start as soon as the teeth come into the mouth. When a child is awake, saliva helps wash away foods that can start tooth decay. When a child is sleeping, saliva flow is reduced and sleeping with a bottle allows the bottle's contents to slowly bathe the teeth for long periods of time.

Baby-bottle tooth decay can occur rapidly and cause the infant unnecessary pain and suffering. The upper front teeth are the ones most likely to be attacked.

The main causes of baby-bottle tooth decay are sugary liquids used for long periods of time — these include milk, formula, fruit juices, and other sweetened liquids such as soft drinks.

Baby-bottle tooth decay can be prevented by:
• cleaning your child's teeth daily,
• giving only plain water in sleep-time bottles,
• giving plain water when your child is thirsty instead of sweetened drinks, and
• beginning to wean your child from the bottle near to your child's first birthday. At this time, teach your child to drink directly from a cup.

Thumb Sucking and Soothers

Sucking is a natural reflex that helps your baby relax and feel secure. Usually the need for sucking diminishes after the age of two or three. Prolonged and vigorous thumb or finger sucking after the age of five, however, can cause problems with the position of developing teeth. If thumb or finger sucking stops before the permanent front teeth come in, the long term effect is usually limited.

If required, use of an orthodontic one-piece soother is encouraged. It should have a small nipple. Breaking the habit of sucking a soother is much easier than breaking a thumb-sucking habit. If you use a pacifier or soother to comfort your child, this should always be clean — only use one recommended by your baby's doctor, dentist, or public health nurse.

Never dip the pacifier in any sweet substance such as honey or syrup.

Teething

Once teething starts, it continues almost uninterrupted for about two years. Each child has his or her own schedule for cutting teeth. Expect the first tooth to come through when your baby is about six months old (see the chart on p. 100 for details). Some babies seem to have no problem with teething while others may become fussy or may not feel like eating. Fever is not related to teething and should be checked by your doctor.

Some things you can do to relieve sore or tender gums:
• Give your baby a clean, chilled teething ring to chew on. Teething cookies or biscuits are not a good choice as they contain sugar and may lead to tooth decay.
• Teething gels or ointment *should only be used* on the advice of your dentist.
• Extra love and patience will help your baby through the teething process.

Visits to the Dentist

Regular dental check-ups should begin once your baby has the first 20 teeth, usually by the age of three years. (A FREE dental consultation is available in British Columbia through the "First Dental Visit Program." B.C. residents will find a coupon inside the cover of the Child Health Passport.) On a first dental visit expect the dentist to have a quick look around the child's mouth, and to receive information on nutrition and ways to care for your child's teeth.

Fluoride

Fluoride is an effective and inexpensive way to prevent tooth decay. If your community has fluoridated water, this is providing a very good method of helping to prevent tooth decay.

Fluoride supplements are now not deemed to be necessary for any child before the age of three years. You should talk with your dentist, family doctor, or public health nurse about fluoride supplements when your child reaches this age (three years old).

All infants will benefit from fluoride toothpaste irrespective of whether or not you have fluoride in your drinking water.

Fluoride-containing toothpastes can be used once per day initially, starting shortly after the first teeth appear in the mouth (about six months of age for the front teeth) by placing a small "smear" of paste on a damp washcloth or gauze pad to gently clean your baby's teeth. When most

of your child's teeth have appeared — about one and a half to two years of age — start gently brushing your child's teeth at least once a day with a small soft toothbrush and a small amount of toothpaste (see illustration). It is best to brush your child's teeth just before bedtime.

Dentists also recommend that parents supervise the tooth brushing of all children under six years of age, discouraging a child from swallowing the pastes used.

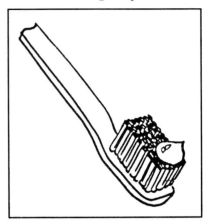

A "pea-sized" amount of fluoride toothpaste should be used. This is the recommended size — more is *not* better. Tooth brushing should be supervised up to the sixth birthday.

First Teeth	When teeth "come in"	When teeth *"fall out"*
Upper		
Central incisors	7-12 mos.	*6-8 yrs.*
Lateral incisors	9-13 mos.	*7-8 yrs.*
Canines (cuspids)	16-22 mos.	*10-12 yrs.*
First molars	13-19 mos.	*9-11 yrs.*
Second molars	25-33 mos.	*10-12 yrs.*
Lower		
Second molars	20-31 mos.	*10-12 yrs.*
First molars	12-18 mos.	*9-11 yrs.*
Canines (cuspids)	16-23 mos.	*9-12 yrs.*
Lateral incisors	7-16 mos.	*7-8 yrs.*
Central incisors	6-10 mos.	*6-8 yrs.*

CODY

Babysitters: Things to Keep in Mind

CARNES

As a parent, it's up to you to decide how soon you leave your baby for an evening out to visit with friends. There's no reason not to leave an infant in the care of a babysitter right from birth if you feel secure about it, as long as you choose your babysitter carefully.

So rather than staying home night after night, declining invitations in favour of television reruns, do yourself a favour: find some reliable babysitters. You can start by contacting:
- trusted friends and neighbours,
- high-school counsellors or child-care instructors,
- the "Y,"
- senior citizens' organizations,
- recreation centres, and
- the sitters' directory at your local community centre (many community centres offer babysitting courses).

Interview potential babysitters, obtain references (at least two), and draw up a list of reliable babysitters that you can call on. The next time you have an appointment or want to do some work, go shopping, or do some errands, you'll have a variety of people to choose from. And who knows — spending an evening alone together, free of the responsibilities of the 24-hour-a-day job of parenting, could become habit-forming!

Even at three months, it is best that the baby be awake when the babysitter arrives. This is important so that the sitter can see how you hold, handle, and care for the baby. Even young babies like to be treated in a way that's familiar to them. Show your babysitter where things are kept, and watch closely as he or she feeds and diapers the baby. You will then be sure the sitter cares about the baby and knows what he or she is doing.

Be clear with your sitter about your expectations regarding care and attention to your child (e.g., let your sitter know how often you want your child checked when sleeping and ask the sitter to limit the length of telephone calls, even when the baby is sleeping).

In order to make the babysitter's job easier, and to make you feel more confident leaving your child in his or her care, you should make sure to leave the following information:

Where you are going, when you expect to return, and how you can be reached.

Emergency telephone numbers:
- Fire: _____
- Police: _____
- Poison Information: _____
- Doctor: _____
- Hospital (pediatric emergency number): _____
- Helpful neighbours (name and number): _____
- Closest relative: _____
- Taxi: _____

Be sure to write down your house address and family name on a piece of paper near the telephone in case the babysitter needs quick access to this information in an emergency.

Information about your child:
- Meal and/or snack times (and preferences)
- Bath time (and routines)
- Bedtime and/or naptime (and routines)
- Play (favourite toys and games)
- Special instructions (allergies, etc.)

Professional Child Care — What to Look For

DECOSTE

If you're like many parents, you may find it very difficult to even think of having anyone look after your child on a regular basis except yourselves or perhaps a close relative. Such caution is understandable; however, if it is carried too far, it could overtax the goodwill of grandparents or other family members. Also, the realities of life are such that sooner or later your child will come under someone else's supervision.

If you choose child care out of your home, you should be aware that the facility must be licensed if more than two children (unrelated to the caregiver) are receiving care. Licensing requirements govern space, hours of care, qualifications of staff, and the ages and number of children allowed. In selecting day care, you should also look for facilities in which you:
• can see the licence displayed,
• can enter at any time of day,
• are allowed to visit all areas,
• can be sure your child is safe and happy,
• feel the staff genuinely like children and provide an enriching environment,
• feel free to have regular talks with the caregiver to discuss the child's progress and accomplishments,
• see evidence of play materials appropriate to your child's age,
• feel the disciplinary methods are appropriate,
• see that change areas are kept clean,
• are asked about the baby's health and immunization status,
• are asked to indicate in writing who can take the child home, and
• are asked to indicate in writing how you can be reached in an emergency and who should be contacted if you can't be reached.

If you choose to have care provided in your home, you should be equally selective. You can find possible candidates through a placement agency, Employment and Immigration Canada, or the newspaper. The applicants should be asked for references from previous employers. They should also be interviewed at least twice to obtain such information as:

• education,
• previous work experience, including ages of children cared for, dates of previous jobs, and reason(s) for leaving,
• current health and lifestyle (e.g., a non-smoker),
• attitudes about child rearing (e.g., discipline, play, toys, nutrition, siblings, etc.), and
• attitude towards and ability to deal with emergencies (e.g., fire, poisoning, choking); medications; other family members (e.g., grandparents); religious and cultural practices; and pets.

Responsibilities of the job will need to be discussed and later agreed upon in writing. Some items you will want to cover are:
• hours and days of child care — allowing a few minutes each day for parent and caregiver to exchange information,
• activities with the baby and the other children (e.g., feeding, bathing, going for walks, use of toys),
• coping with such behaviour as crying, thumb sucking, aggressiveness,
• housekeeping duties (e.g., laundry, cooking, light or heavy house cleaning),
• management of emergencies, sickness, and first aid, and
• baby safety.

Benefits and working conditions also need to be discussed and agreed upon in writing:
• salary and payment procedures,
• non-financial benefits (e.g., coffee breaks, trips with family),
• amount of paid vacation and sick leave, and
• review of employee's work performance.

You can obtain further information about employee benefits and working conditions from Revenue Canada and Employment and Immigration Canada. See also the article "A Guide to Further Resources" at the back of this handbook.

Baby and Me Alone

If you are single, parenting on your own can be both challenging and rewarding. Single parents have said: "People often put a lot of pressure on me to do things their way."

"Buy baby supplies ahead of time."

"Look for a weekly mothers' support group!"

"Don't feel bad to take help from others."

"Talk over living arrangements carefully before moving in with parents or other friends — they may not have the same 'parenting rules' as you."

"If you are a single parent, make sure you *always* have someone to talk to. It's really important not to keep things inside. It can be helpful for both you and your child to talk your problems out."

"Don't live your life just for your child. Single parents need time for themselves to relax and enjoy life. If you are happy, your child will be happier."

"Don't overcompensate for the lack of the other parent. A child who has no limits is hard to take care of."

When you are facing single parenthood, finding people and programs to support you is very important. To find the appropriate resources and support, contact a public health nurse at your local health unit/department. The public health nurse can help you find information about prenatal education or classes you feel comfortable with. Regular visits to your doctor, beginning early in your pregnancy, are also important. If you don't have a doctor, discuss how to find one with the public health nurse or a social worker. Also see the article "Choosing a Health Care Provider" on p. 8 for some hints on how to find the right doctor for you.

At times, some single mothers find that they need special support and advice.

Money

If you find yourself in need of financial advice or advice on how to establish paternity and claims for maintenance, ask a social worker or a public health nurse to refer you to the appropriate provincial government agency or ministry. Local offices of provincial agencies and ministries are listed in the blue pages of your telephone directory.

Living Arrangements

Finding housing that provides some personal support while easing financial pressures is important. Many communities have a housing information network, co-op housing, etc. Check with community services, a social worker, or a public health nurse.

Time for Yourself

Many recreation programs have child-care exchanges or on-site care available. Check with a public health nurse for pamphlets on single parent resources as well as how to find reliable child care.

Who Can Help You?

You are the best person to make decisions for yourself and your child. However, sometimes you may need to talk to someone who understands the challenges of single parenting. Talking to other single parents and getting support from friends and family can be helpful. Contact your community services agency or a public health nurse for information about parent support groups in your area.

Returning to School or Work

If you are considering returning to school or work, your local school district or college can provide information on options for furthering your education. Contact Employment and Immigration Canada about child-related benefits and job re-entry programs (see the blue pages of your telephone directory).

A Social Life

Social events hosted by libraries, friendship centres, churches, moms and tots groups, local recreation centres, or the "Y" can provide you and your child with some relaxation and give you opportunities to meet new people.

Dealing with Problems

Everyone needs help to handle loneliness, stress, relationships, child behaviour, sleeping problems, or substance abuse, at various points in their lives. Talk to someone who can help you. Your doctor, a local public health nurse, or a social worker may have some helpful ideas.

For more information on how to find people and programs to support you, see the article "A Guide to Further Resources" at the back of this handbook.

Getting through the Day as a New Mother

Many new mothers feel completely unprepared for the changes a baby makes in their lives. "No one told me it would be like this" is a common complaint. One reason for this is that expectant mothers are so busy coping with the demands of pregnancy and preparing for the birth that any thought of what life might be like after the baby is born is the furthest thing from their minds. They may not be ready to discuss changes that, to some extent, need to be experienced to be understood.

But ready or not, many women realize that having some idea of what to expect will help them adjust to the presence of a new baby. Even if you're mainly concerned about what to take to the hospital, or how to recognize the early signs of labour, the information about what having a new baby might be like can be filed away until you need it. *Baby's Best Chance* obtained this information from the best of all possible sources — the new mothers themselves. We interviewed a group of new mothers with babies ranging in age from six weeks to five months. Their experiences may not match your own, since everyone's situation is unique. However, reading their words and remembering them later will help you realize that as a new mother you won't be alone. You will be part of a community of women who experience many of the same joys and frustrations.

What You're Up Against

"The first week after coming home from the hospital, I felt like curling up into a little ball. The baby would cry in one corner and I'd cry in the other corner. That's what we'd do all day. Thank goodness that didn't last long. Now that my son is six weeks old, I feel like I've gotten back to normal."

"The first couple of weeks were a hard adjustment. I didn't think I'd be able to handle it. Some days I felt like saying, 'Somebody take this baby away. I don't want it!'"

"During pregnancy, I was so elated you couldn't wipe the smile off my face. During the first week after my daughter

was born, I was still floating on cloud nine. The thrill of this wonderful, beautiful baby held me over that first week. By the second week, the exhaustion took over. Then it was an uphill climb every day. There were many days that it was the middle of the afternoon and I still didn't have my teeth brushed."

"I come from a professional background, incredibly organized, always have been. Then I got thrown into this new life where nothing is predictable."

"The reality is that if you have a baby in your thirties, you don't have the same energy level."

"Listen, I'm 25 and I feel the same way."

"We were married for six years before we decided to have a family, and we were very set in our routine as a couple. We're really finding it difficult now. There's this new person, and this person is taking up all of our time."

"I think the person who said babies are supposed to meld into your lives is the same person who said babies should sleep 20 hours a day!"

"Mothers are never honest, right? Because if they were, we'd never have babies. (LAUGHS) I was told that newborns are wonderful, and all they do is eat and sleep. So I figured I'd have all this time off to do all kinds of other things. But no one told me that they cry all the rest of the time. At least that was what my baby did. I found it very hard to convince myself that I wasn't inadequate and I wasn't the only person going through this."

"I came from a job where I ran a department of 25 people. How could I get that many people organized when I couldn't get one person organized? It took me a long time to get over the feeling that I was a problem. I had a lot of trying days."

"The first few weeks you're home, everybody in town knows you've just had a baby — baby shoe bronzers, vacuum cleaner salesmen, you name it — and they all phone and try to sell you something."

Time for Yourself

"I'd sell my kid to the highest bidder sometimes just to have a few hours to myself."

"I rush into the shower after putting the baby down for his morning nap, but usually he's screaming by the time I step out of the shower. And I'd think, 'Oh God! I shouldn't have conditioned my hair!'"

"I used to always wear nail polish, but since the baby came there's no way. I didn't even curl my hair and wear make-up until after she was six weeks old."

"People talk about going out and shopping as being a break, but I find it a chore. You go to the drugstore, you do your banking, you buy groceries, and your two hours are up and you have to go home and feed the baby. Remember the good old days when you used to window shop and look at all the new clothes and try on the odd thing? Well, forget it!"

Routines

"I find that once five o'clock in the afternoon rolls around, I'm dead on my feet. All I want to do is get dinner out of the way and then collapse."

"It's really gotten a lot better since he started sleeping through the night."

"It's hard to wake up at four o'clock in the morning to feed the baby if you're not used to it, especially after being off work and home for the last few months of pregnancy and napping during the day."

"My baby sleeps from nine in the evening until three in the morning, but if you ask me if my baby sleeps through the night, I'll say no. It may be six hours, but how many of us go to bed at nine at night?"

Husbands/Partners

"Neither my husband nor I are used to little children. We hadn't been around them much. I've adjusted to having Anthony because I'm with him all day long, but even after six and a half weeks, my husband still isn't used to him. If the baby isn't fed right on schedule, he gets upset."

"It's hard for husbands to know what it's like. I mean, he'll come home from work at five o'clock and ask me what I did today. I'll tell him I looked after the baby and he'll say, 'Is that all?' Then he'll ask, 'What's for dinner tonight?' and I'll tell him to look in the oven and if anything's there, that's dinner."

"They don't really see how much work it is being a new mother and how it takes up all your time all day long."

"The baby was waking my husband up and he had to go to work, so I would sleep some of the time in the baby's room. I told my mother I was doing that and she said she'd be out right away! She thought that meant Divorce City!"

"My baby's only seven weeks old and I know this will change, but I find I really miss that intimate relationship with my husband."

"We went out twice after the baby was born, just for a couple of hours in the evening. The baby was staying with relatives so there was no problem. Well, my husband just couldn't get used to that idea. He felt like he was abandoning the baby. I see the baby all day long so I didn't feel guilty at all!"

Friends

"Sometimes I feel like it's me and my baby and that's it."

"A lot of my friends would say, 'What's there to having a baby? People've been having babies for thousands of years. It's no big deal!' That would make me feel like I wasn't doing a good job, and I must be the only one who doesn't know how to do this. I'm over that now!"

"It was like I was an invalid when I was pregnant and I really didn't need the attention then. I needed the attention after the baby was born! Everyone rushed to see the new baby, and now it's like all my friends have forgotten me! I find that kind of hard to deal with. And then people don't want to phone you because they don't know if you're sleeping or feeding the baby or whatever. My son's going to be five months old in a couple of weeks and only now am I starting to get in touch with people again."

"One of my friends gave me the most incredible gift I could have ever gotten and that was maid service. I'd go out with the baby for two hours and I'd come home to this beautiful clean house — everything polished. It was great!"

"Another good idea for a gift is a month or whatever of diaper service."

"The best thing a friend can give you is a dinner that you can heat up and put on the table. I never thought I'd like casseroles. Now I'd give my eye teeth for a casserole."

"One of my friends gave me a big bag of crackers, fruit, you name it. For the first couple of weeks, all I had to do was go to the fridge and there it was. I think that was the most wonderful thing I got."

Going Back to Work

"I think we're living with our mothers' ideals of how things should be. The trouble is, they didn't work outside the home and most of us have to."

"I've changed my back-to-work date three times."

"I'm going back to work in six weeks and I find I'm so unorganized still. There's no schedule with this baby. As a newborn, he slept through the night. Now he's up three times a night. I'm in a real panic because I'm going to have to get up at five in the morning to get ready to go to work!"

"When I have to go back to work, to help alleviate those awful feelings, I'm going to get myself a new outfit for the first day back."

"I went out a couple of times and left my baby with the babysitter before going back to work, to see how my baby would cope. I found that worked really well. I could go back to work knowing my baby was O.K."

"I didn't think it would be possible to nurse and go back to work, so I weaned my baby last month. That was another whole set of emotions. I felt terrible! I'd give her the bottle and she'd turn to me instead. Well, that was it, I just cried! But she was fine, she took the bottle fine. It was nothing to her as long as she was getting fed."

A Few Thoughts for Mothers or Mothers-to-be

"If anyone offers help, take it. Don't be proud!"

"One of the best things we did was to get a little lambskin for our baby to sleep on. He quickly became attached to his 'sheepy' and actually preferred cuddling with it to cuddling his stuffed toys. Whenever we needed to be away from home at naptime, we simply took along the lambskin, and he would go happily to bed, despite the unfamiliar surroundings. We could always count on the lambskin to help keep him warm, even when he kicked off his blankets."

"Make arrangements to go for a walk even for half an hour by yourself, if you can. Leave the baby with Dad for awhile. You feel guilty and it's hard to do, but if you can do that, you'll survive."

"Learn to say no so that when other people say you've had all afternoon with the baby and just pack up your diaper bag and come visit, you can say no — that you're really tired and need to lay low."

"Being a parent is like learning to ride a bicycle. How many of us knew how to ride a bicycle right away? The reality is babies are very flexible. They love you so much and you may make all sorts of mistakes, but as long as it's done in love, they'll survive."

"It's critical that you don't be concerned about your housework and meals. As long as you get your nutrition, who cares if it's out of a can? Just keep in mind that those things are going to happen — you're going to have a dirty house, a messy kitchen, and no gourmet meals for a couple of months."

"I don't think women have to worry that much about breastfeeding. I think breastfeeding's great, but I also supplement with a bottle and my baby and I are doing fine. I don't think women should feel guilty."

"When it comes to looking after your baby, whatever feels right for you, do it. If you start doing things because someone else tells you to, you're in trouble. Throw the rules out the window!"

Infant Care: Some Common Concerns

The following information addresses some of the common concerns new parents have about their babies. If you have any further questions related to the subjects discussed here, contact your doctor or a public health nurse.

Normal Bowel Movements

For the first week after birth, the appearance of your baby's stools will change every day.

Your baby's first bowel movement will probably occur between 8 and 24 hours after birth. He or she will pass a sticky, odourless material that is greenish-black or brownish-green. This is called "meconium." By the third to fifth day, your baby's stools will be loose and greenish-yellow. The stools will also contain mucus.

After that, the appearance of the stools depends on what you feed your baby. Babies who are completely breastfed will have stools that vary from dark brown or green to mustard or yellow. The stools may also be soft and runny with a curdled or seed-like appearance. The frequency of bowel movements will also vary. Stools may be passed after every feeding or only once every few days. For the first few weeks, a baby's elimination may be fairly explosive and the stool may be loose and liquid. This is normal.

Bottlefed babies who are on formula may have firm, light yellow stools. These babies may have one or two bowel movements daily. With some types of formula, your baby may have stools very similar to those of breastfed babies.

When your baby starts to eat solid food, the bowel movements will become brown-coloured and firmer and may be less frequent. Again, the colour and frequency will depend on the type of food eaten.

Diarrhea

Diarrhea is often caused by an infection in the baby's intestines. The infection may be a result of germs from a feeding bottle, food, or contact with another person. Diarrhea may also be the result of some other illness or irritation.

When a baby has diarrhea, the stools are more frequent than usual. They are watery and foul-smelling. The stools may also be expelled with considerable force. Your baby's tummy may protrude and be tight to the touch. He or she may refuse to eat or may even vomit.

If you breastfeed your baby, continue feeding as usual. If your baby is bottlefed, a temporary change in formula may be necessary or a commercial oral rehydration solution (for no longer than 24 hours). Consult your doctor for advice.

Constipation

Newborn babies normally grunt, get red in the face, and grimace when having a bowel movement. Thus, there is no reason to think your baby is constipated unless stools are dry and hard and your baby has difficulty passing them. How often your baby has a bowel movement is less important than how the stools look.

A baby who is completely breastfed rarely gets constipated, since breast milk is almost totally digested. After the first few weeks, a fully breastfed baby may go as long as a week between bowel movements. Baby's bowel habits may change slightly when solids are first introduced. This is common and no cause for concern. If you feel that your baby is constipated, discuss this with your public health nurse.

If constipation continues for more than a week, or if there is fresh blood in the baby's stools, consult your doctor. Do not use laxatives, suppositories, or enemas unless they are prescribed by your doctor.

Urination

Babies are born with urine in the bladder. Your baby may pass water either immediately after birth or several hours later. Since your baby's kidneys are immature, the urine will be pale. Also, it is not unusual to find a pink stain on the diapers.

Six or more wet diapers of pale urine over 24 hours (four or more disposable diapers) indicate that your baby is getting enough to drink.

Hiccoughs

Many babies have frequent attacks of hiccoughs, which can be quite loud and explosive. Often, hiccoughs bother the parents more than they seem to bother the baby. Hiccoughs usually go away as food digests in the stomach. Sometimes a small drink or a change of position can help.

Spitting Up and Vomiting

Spitting up small amounts after a meal is very common in the first few months of life and is not the same as vomiting. As a baby's digestive system matures and becomes more efficient, he or she will outgrow the spitting up. As long as your baby is well and does not appear hungry, spitting up should not be a matter for concern. Young babies can be placed on their side with a small, rolled towel behind to support their back when not being held. This may help prevent choking. The side a newborn lies on should be alternated. The Canadian Pediatric Society recommends that healthy, full-term infants be placed on their backs or their sides for sleep.

Bouts of vomiting occur less frequently than spitting up. Vomiting involves the forceful throwing up of large amounts of liquid or food, is usually associated with an illness, and can lead to dehydration. Consult your doctor immediately if vomiting continues.

Coughing and Sneezing

Coughing and sneezing is common in newborns. They are unable to blow their nose, so this is how they clear their nasal passages. A humidifier may help. It is uncommon for a newborn to develop a cold within the first six weeks. However, if you are concerned, check with your doctor.

Keeping Your Baby at a Comfortable Temperature

Babies, like adults, enjoy feeling comfortably warm. This means an indoor temperature of approximately 22°C (71.6°F) and no drafts. When your home is cooler, provide an extra sweater or booties.

Babies do not sweat efficiently so they can become dangerously overheated. For this reason, an electric blanket, heating pad, or hot water bottle should never be used. In summer, when the weather is warm, dress your baby in lightweight, loose clothes. This will help sweat evaporate off the skin and keep your baby comfortable.

There are many opinions about when a baby should go outside. In deciding what to do, keep in mind that a baby's skin is very sensitive. In summer, keep your baby in a cool, shady spot. Also, protect his or her eyes and head with a sun hat. Doctors recommend that babies under one year of age should be kept entirely out of direct sunlight. Sunscreen is not to be used with infants under six months of age, as it will not provide adequate protection to their easily damaged skin. If insects are around, protect your baby by covering the carriage or basket with a fine netting.

In winter, shelter your baby from damp, cold air, which tends to be chilling. Provide your baby with extra blankets below as well as on top. When outside, make sure that your baby is wearing a hood or bonnet. Keep any exposure to extreme cold very brief. Check with your public health nurse for more information.

How to Take Your Baby's Temperature

It is important to know how to take your baby's temperature if you think he or she is running a fever. To do this, place a thermometer under the baby's armpit for five minutes. A normal temperature is between 36 and 37°C (96.8 and 98.6°F). If your baby's temperature is 38°C (100.4°F) or over, contact your doctor.

Planning the Rest of Your Family

If you are like most people, you are probably not inclined to give much thought to family planning and birth control during the last few weeks of pregnancy and the first few weeks following the birth of your baby. Yet it is important to consider these matters now. Pregnancy, childbirth, and infant care make enormous demands on a woman's physical resources. This means that becoming pregnant again soon after the birth of one child could endanger her health. It could also affect the health of that next child.

If you are planning to have more children, it is a good idea to space the births so that two or three years elapse between pregnancies. This will allow time for the mother's body to regain its resources before she becomes pregnant again. It will also increase the chances that she and the baby will be in good health. Also, other children in the family will be able to anticipate the arrival of the baby, having had a chance to develop a secure relationship with each parent.

Keep in mind, therefore, that once you resume sexual activity, conception can occur as early as four to six weeks after the birth, even if you are breastfeeding (see the article "And What about Sex?" on p. 29). Women who do breastfeed will usually not have their first period until later; however, this cannot be relied on as a way of preventing pregnancy. It is impossible to predict when the mild contraceptive effect of breastfeeding will wear off and the first postpartum menstrual period will occur. Also, ovulation occurs before that first period, so conception can take place before a woman is even aware she is fertile again.

To prevent pregnancy, using an effective method of birth control is a must. Douching after intercourse will not work. Withdrawal (i.e., when the man withdraws his penis from the vagina before orgasm) is also not an effective method. Fortunately, there are several proven methods to choose from. A description of what is involved in each method is included in the following summary chart.

Pregnancy Prevention

The only 100 per cent effective way of avoiding pregnancy is to not have intercourse. If that is not an option for you, here are some alternatives to consider.

Method	How it is used
Condom	The condom is worn on the penis to stop sperm from entering the vagina. Several types (made from either latex or natural membrane) are available. Following ejaculation, the condom must be held carefully in order to prevent spillage of semen while the penis is removed from the vagina. If lubrication is needed, use a spermicide. A condom should never be used more than once. Also, condoms may be damaged by rough treatment and can deteriorate if exposed to direct sunlight, fluorescent light, or heat for long periods of time (e.g., kept in wallet in pants pocket).
Diaphragm or Cervical Cap	The diaphragm or cervical cap should be prescribed and fitted by a doctor. It is inserted into the vagina and placed over the cervix to stop sperm from entering the uterus. To be effective, it must be used with a spermicide and must be left in place six to eight hours following intercourse. For repeat intercourse, more spermicide should be added (for diaphragm only). Both should be cleaned carefully with soap and warm water upon removal and examined for small punctures or tears (examine it by holding it up to light). Diaphragms may last for up to two years, but cervical caps should be replaced yearly.
Morning-After Pill	The morning-after pill is an emergency method of birth control that can be used after unprotected or unexpected intercourse, if a condom breaks, or if a diaphragm or cervical cap becomes dislodged.
Spermicides	Spermicides work by making a sperm-killing barrier inside the vagina. Various types are available: foam, jelly, and tablets. Their effectiveness is increased when used with a condom, diaphragm, or cervical cap.
Fertility Awareness	Fertility awareness involves knowing which days in a woman's cycle are her fertile days. Intercourse is then avoided during those "unsafe" days. Various symptoms (e.g., body temperature, condition of cervical mucus) are observed and recorded to determine when a woman is fertile. Four main methods include (1) the basal body temperature method, (2) the calendar method, (3) the mucus method, and (4) the sympto-thermal method. Special training from a qualified counsellor is required to learn how to use fertility awareness methods. Contact your doctor or local public health nurse for information.
IUD	There are various types of IUD. All are essentially a small, flexible piece of sterile plastic (with copper or medication) inserted into the uterus. An IUD must be inserted by a doctor. A small string descending into the vagina allows the woman to check the IUD's position after each period. IUDs appear to work primarily by preventing fertilization of the egg.
"The Pill"	There are several different types of birth-control pills available. They all work by releasing a dose of hormone that prevents ovulation. A woman must take one pill regularly as prescribed by her doctor. Missing one or more pills can result in loss of protection. If this occurs, the advice of a doctor or other qualified health professional should be sought and a temporary, alternative method used. A woman should never use someone else's pills. Because antibiotics cause birth-control pills to be less effective, a woman receiving a prescription for antibiotics while on birth-control pills should discuss this reduced effectiveness with her doctor.
Male Sterilization (Vasectomy)	The tubes carrying sperm from the testes (vas deferens) are cut or sealed so that sperm cannot pass. The operation is considered minor and is performed under local anaesthetic. The man still produces semen, and his ability to ejaculate and enjoy intercourse are not affected. Follow-up visits to the doctor ensure the man is fully sterile. This operation is generally covered by provincial medical plans.
Female Sterilization (Tubal Occlusion)	The tubes that carry the egg to the uterus (fallopian tubes) are cut or sealed so the egg cannot pass. The operation may be performed under local or general anaesthetic. The woman's ability to have and enjoy intercourse is unaffected. This operation is generally covered by provincial medical plans.
Contraceptive Sponge	The contraceptive sponge is a disposable, single-use polyurethane sponge containing spermicide. It must be moistened with water prior to insertion. Placed over the cervix, it acts both as a barrier and a spermicide. The contraceptive sponge must be left in place for six hours following intercourse.

Method	How it is used
Norplant	Norplant consists of six small, soft capsules which are placed under the skin of the woman's upper arm through a small incision using local anaesthetic. It provides five years of low dose, progestin-only contraception. Norplant can be inserted six weeks after childbirth or within seven days after the start of a period.
Depo-Provera	In 1992, the United States Food and Drug Administration approved the use of Depo-Provera for contraception in the United States. This drug is an injectable contraceptive which is effective for three months. It is approved for therapeutic use but not for contraception in Canada; however, physicians may prescribe a drug for an unapproved purpose if they feel it is appropriate for a particular patient and provided the patient receives adequate information to give informed consent about the drug.
Female Condom	The Female Condom is a soft, loose-fitting polyurethane vaginal sheath worn by women to provide protection from unintended pregnancy and sexually transmitted diseases (STDs). It is a disposable, single-use device which is held in place by a flexible, outer ring that covers the vulva and a loose, inner ring that is placed inside the vagina.

Advantages

Condom
- can be bought without a prescription
- latex condoms: reduce the risk of contracting sexually transmitted diseases (STDs), including AIDS
- allows birth control responsibility to be shared
- no side effects
- 90 to 98 per cent effective

Diaphragm or Cervical Cap
- cannot be felt by either partner
- used only when needed
- no serious side effects
- diaphragm: 87 to 98 per cent effective with spermicide
- cervical cap: 84 to 97 per cent effective with spermicide

Morning-After Pill
- 98 to 99 per cent effective if taken within 72 hours of unprotected intercourse

Spermicides
- can be bought without a prescription
- have no serious side effects
- can't be felt except for extra moisture
- 70 to 85 per cent effective

Fertility Awareness
- acceptable to religious groups that do not approve of other methods
- promotes understanding of the reproductive system
- can enhance communication for some couples
- can be used either to plan or to avoid pregnancy
- no side effects
- 70 to 98 per cent effective, depending on method or combination of methods used

IUD
- continuous protection
- no interference with lovemaking
- can be left in place for 30 months or longer
- 97 to 99 per cent effective

Disadvantages

Condom
- must be unwrapped and put on erect penis prior to genital contact
- must be used correctly for each act of intercourse

Diaphragm or Cervical Cap
- must be inserted before intercourse
- can cause discomfort if not inserted properly
- more chance of bladder infections
- must be left in place at least 6 and no more than 24 hours following intercourse (cervical cap is 48 hours)
- effectiveness reduced if used incorrectly
- must not be used during menstruation

Morning-After Pill
- requires doctor's prescription
- must not be used more than once in any cycle
- may cause short-term nausea, temporary cycle disruption

Spermicides
- new dose must be inserted shortly before each act of intercourse
- some users are sensitive or allergic to products
- can be confused with feminine hygiene products

Fertility Awareness
- may be impractical for couples not in a committed, co-operative relationship
- charting of indicators must be accurate

IUD
- more painful cramps during periods for some women
- increased risk of pelvic inflammatory disease if a sexually transmitted disease is contracted
- can be dislodged during menstrual periods

Advantages	Disadvantages
"The Pill" • most effective of the reversible methods • convenient and easy to use • no unpleasant side effects for most women • lighter menstrual flow; less cramping • may lower the risk of cancer of the ovaries, uterus, and some breast diseases • 98 to 99 per cent effective	**"The Pill"** • requires doctor's prescription • some minor side effects for some women • should not be taken by women who smoke or have certain medical conditions (e.g., heart condition, high blood pressure, circulatory problems, active liver disease, breast cancer) • Cigarette smoking increases the risk of serious adverse effects on the heart and blood vessels. This risk increases with age and becomes significant in pill users over 35 years of age.
Male Sterilization • fear of pregnancy eliminated • almost 100 per cent effective	**Male Sterilization** • should be considered irreversible and is not appropriate for young persons • some slight chance of complication due to surgery
Female Sterilization • fear of pregnancy eliminated • almost 100 per cent effective	**Female Sterilization** • should be considered irreversible and is not appropriate for young persons • some slight chance of complication due to surgery
Contraceptive Sponge • can be bought without a prescription • can be left in place, providing continuous contraception for 24 hours • 85 per cent effective	**Contraceptive Sponge** • some users are sensitive or allergic to spermicide • must not be used within six weeks of end of pregnancy, nor during vaginal bleeding from any cause, including menstruation
Norplant • can be used by breastfeeding women • fertility returns soon after the capsules are taken out • nothing to remember to do before sex • no daily motivation is required • 99.8% effective	**Norplant** • requires minor surgical procedure for insertion and removal • irregular menstrual bleeding; longer periods; spotting; no periods • some women experience headaches • possible side effects include mood changes, weight gain or loss, fluid retention, and aggravation of acne • cost may be a factor (currently $450 to $500 in the USA)
Depo-Provera • doesn't contain estrogen; can be used by women with hypertension and smokers over 35 years of age • can be used when breastfeeding; doesn't interfere with milk production • can be used by women who can't take birth-control pills because they are on other medication that may interfere with the birth-control pill's effectiveness • 99.6% effective	**Depo-Provera** • return to fertility may be delayed • irregular bleeding occurs in about 1/3 of users in the first year • headaches, dizziness, bloating of the abdomen or breasts, and mood changes occur in some women
Female Condom • will be available without prescription • comes prelubricated; comfortable to use; transmits heat • can be inserted well in advance of intercourse • made of a thin, strong, tear-resistant material • 74% effective	**Female Condom** • the outer ring extends outside the vagina • requires insertion • can be noisy during intercourse • can be awkward to use

Changes brought about in a woman's body as a result of childbirth may mean a previously used method is no longer reliable. Some methods cannot be started until at least six weeks after the birth of your baby. If you intend to resume sexual relations earlier, discuss your options with your doctor or public health nurse.

Each woman interested in the use of the birth-control pill while breastfeeding should discuss this with her doctor. The hormones contained in these low dosage pills are passed into the breast milk in small quantities, but do not seem to alter its quality or volume as long as the pills are not taken before breastfeeding is well established (four to six weeks after delivery). The long-term effects of the hormones transmitted are not known.

In choosing a method of birth control, you may wish to consider the following:
• how easy it is to use correctly,
• how much it costs to use this method,
• how you and your partner feel about the method,
• whether you or your partner have more than one partner. If so, you should consider using a *latex* condom to reduce the risk of AIDS or other sexually transmitted diseases. The addition of a spermicide can increase protection, but only if it is non-irritating to you.

111

A Guide to Further Resources

Alcohol and Drug Information

- All provinces and territories have programs for people with alcohol and other drug problems. Ask your health care professional, or check in the yellow pages under "Alcohol" or "Drug" information. Residents of British Columbia can also call the Ministry of Health's Alcohol and Drug Referral Service (1-800-663-1441) — a confidential, toll-free information line to alcohol and other drug programs in the province.
- For smoking, a self-help program is available from your local lung association, listed in the white pages of your telephone directory.

Children with Disabilities

- There are provincial services available if your baby has a developmental problem or a disability. Your public health nurse can help you locate these services. Most communities have an Infant Development Program for children from birth to age three. Staff in this program may assist you in providing activities for your baby that will encourage his or her development, and in accessing other supports that may help you and your baby. A diagnosis of a developmental problem for a young child is difficult for any parent, but there are many other parents and professionals to help you at this time and as your child grows older. A child with severe disabilities may be eligible for the benefits of the At Home Program.

Day Care

- For information to help you select a day-care facility for your child and monitor the ongoing level of care your child is receiving, contact your municipal or provincial department of Social Services. In British Columbia, a Ministry of Health brochure "Parents' Guide to Selecting Day Care" is available at local health units/departments.

Family Violence

- If your pregnancy is more difficult because of family violence, contact your local office of the Ministry of Social Services (see the blue pages in the telephone directory), call the women's helpline or local shelter listed on the inside cover of your telephone directory or in the white pages.

First Aid

- Emergency telephone numbers (e.g., fire, police, ambulance, and poison information centre) are located on the inside cover of your telephone book.
- The Canadian Red Cross Society offers a "ChildSafe" program which teaches basic skills for dealing with emergencies. For more information, contact your local branch of the Red Cross, listed in the white pages under "Canadian Red Cross Society."
- St. John Ambulance offers programs in first aid, C.P.R., and child care. Local branches of St. John Ambulance are listed in the white pages of your telephone directory, and in the Yellow Pages under "First Aid Services."

Infant and Child Car Seats

- For information including rental services in your area, contact your public health nurse.
- Most provincial ministries of transportation have brochures available on child car safety seats; these ministries are listed in the blue pages of your telephone directory. In addition, residents of British Columbia can contact the Insurance Corporation of British Columbia (ICBC) for details on car safety seats. Write to:
  Traffic Safety Education Department, Insurance Corporation of British Columbia, 151 West Esplanade, North Vancouver, B.C., V7M 3H9
- Tether anchor instructions and other information on how to correctly install and use car safety seats is available from most provincial automobile associations. Check in the white pages for the office near you and call or write to request a brochure.

Leave of Absence

- Information on maternal and parental leave of absence is available from the Employment Standards Branch of your provincial Ministry of Labour (listed in the blue pages of your telephone directory).

Medical Genetics Program

- This program is a source of information about genetic or environmental factors that may increase the risk of birth defects in a baby. Discuss this with your doctor if you wish to know more and for referral.

Multiple Births

- Check with your doctor and/or local health unit/department for information on local support groups in your area and the address of "Parents of Multiple Births Association."

Postpartum Depression

- The Pacific Post Partum Support Society has a guide for mothers who are experiencing postpartum depression entitled, *Post Partum Depression and Anxiety: A Self Help Guide for Mothers*. For information about postpartum depression support groups, contact your public health nurse or the Society at the following address:
  Pacific Post Partum Support Society, #104 – 1416 Commercial Drive, Vancouver, B.C., V5L 3X9

Single Parents

- If you require financial advice or advice on claims for maintenance, contact the Ministry of the Attorney General or the Ministry of Social Services. Check the blue pages of your telephone directory for your local community office.
- Parental support groups such as "Parents without Partners" and "Nobody's Perfect" are available in many communities. Contact your local health unit/department, mental health agency, or Ministry of Social Services office about programs available in your community.
- If you are planning to return to school, the Ministry of Social Services may be able to assist you in considering options for furthering your education and planning your career.